Tropical FISH
IDENTIFIER

Tropical*FISH*
IDENTIFIER

A COMPLETE GUIDE TO IDENTIFYING,
CHOOSING, AND KEEPING FRESHWATER
AND MARINE SPECIES

GINA SANDFORD

COURAGE
BOOKS

A QUINTET BOOK

9 8 7 6 5 4 3 2 1
Digit on the right indicates the number of
this printing.

Library of Congress
Cataloging-in-Publication Number
93–72730

ISBN 1–56138–375–9

This book was designed and produced by
Quintet Publishing Limited
6 Blundell Street
London N7 9BH

Creative Director: Richard Dewing
Designer: James Lawrence
Project Editor: Stefanie Foster
Editor: Lydia Darbyshire
Illustrator: Greta Fenton
Photography: Gina and Mike Sandford
Additional photography:
Derek Lambourne, David Allison

Typeset in Great Britain by
Central Southern Typesetters, Eastbourne
Manufactured in Hong Kong
by Regent Publishing Services Limited
Printed in Hong Kong
by Leefung-Asco Printers Limited

Published by Courage Books
an imprint of Running Press Book Publishers
125 South Twenty-second Street
Philadelphia, Pennsylvania 19103-4399

CONTENTS

Directory

INTRODUCTION

Keeping fish is a fascinating and relaxing hobby. Do not be deterred by the many myths surrounding tropical fish – that they are delicate, difficult, expensive, hard to keep and costly to maintain. Nothing could be further from the truth.

With a little research and some careful planning, you can have a focal point in your home that is both educational and beautiful. The fish described in this book range in size from the ¾in Jelly Bean Tetra (*Lepidarchus adonis*) to the 5ft Pacu (*Piaractus brachypomum*). Naturally, these fish could not be housed together, but this is where the research and planning comes in. Freshwater fish are considered easier for the beginner, but, if you have a basic knowledge of fishkeeping, maybe you would like to consider marine fish. You have made a start by buying this book. Read it and see which fish appeal to you, then decide if you can cope with the fish's needs.

The first section deals with the basic requirements of setting up both freshwater and marine aquaria, including lighting, heating, filtration, and water management. It also describes what a fish is and where supplies of aquarium fish come from. If all goes well in the aquarium, you will find yourself consulting the breeding strategies section, and if as happens to all of us at some stage or other, your fish become ill, this aspect is discussed in the fish health section.

In the second section we look at various species. There is a summary of the basic needs of each species together with a short discussion on some points that may help you keep it in peak condition. Where known, a guide to the breeding and raising of fry (the fish's offspring) is included.

Use this work as a guide. When it comes to fishkeeping, all books can only be guides because no two fish are ever exactly the same. Never be afraid to ask questions, regardless of how trivial they may seem to you. Every fishkeeper had to start somewhere, and most specialist outlets are only too willing to help you – although it is best if you can try to pick a relatively quiet time to discuss your needs. There is such a wealth of equipment available these days that it often confuses the experienced aquarist, never mind the beginner!

You will probably also find it helpful to join a local aquarium society. You can find contact addresses in one of the national aquatic magazines or you could visit one of the national shows and make contact with the federation that is organizing it, which will be able to point you in the right direction. You are sure to find that these people are only too willing to help and further your interest in the hobby. Above all, enjoy the hobby.

KEY TO THE SYMBOLS USED WITH EACH ENTRY

Each entry is accompanied by at-a-glance reference symbols, providing an instant overview of the fish being described.

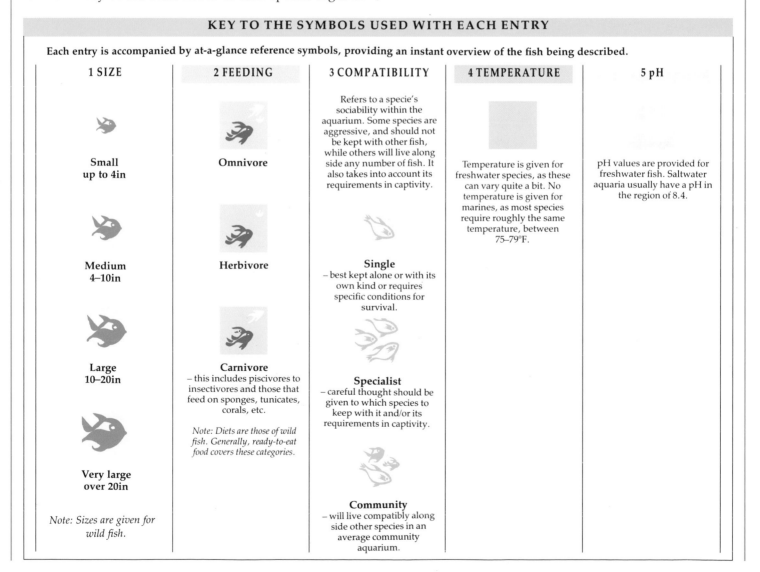

1 SIZE	2 FEEDING	3 COMPATIBILITY	4 TEMPERATURE	5 pH
Small up to 4in	**Omnivore**	Refers to a specie's sociability within the aquarium. Some species are aggressive, and should not be kept with other fish, while others will live along side any number of fish. It also takes into account its requirements in captivity.	Temperature is given for freshwater species, as these can vary quite a bit. No temperature is given for marines, as most species require roughly the same temperature, between 75–79°F.	pH values are provided for freshwater fish. Saltwater aquaria usually have a pH in the region of 8.4.
Medium 4–10in	**Herbivore**	**Single** – best kept alone or with its own kind or requires specific conditions for survival.		
Large 10–20in	**Carnivore** – this includes piscivores to insectivores and those that feed on sponges, tunicates, corals, etc. *Note: Diets are those of wild fish. Generally, ready-to-eat food covers these categories.*	**Specialist** – careful thought should be given to which species to keep with it and/or its requirements in captivity.		
Very large over 20in *Note: Sizes are given for wild fish.*		**Community** – will live compatibly along side other species in an average community aquarium.		

ESTABLISHING *an* AQUARIUM

Fish have existed on this planet for far longer than humans – around 250 million years, compared with the 4 million years that man has existed. This has allowed evolution to hone the physiology and biology of fish to their chosen environment.

UNDERSTANDING FISH

There are more than 30,000 different species of fish known to man, and many more still to be discovered in fresh, brackish, and marine waters. This diversity inevitably means that any explanation of their biology or physiology can be only a generalization. There are always exceptions, which is, perhaps, why fish are so stimulating to observe, breed and keep. Where these exceptions exist (and there are many), you should research in other, more specialized publications.

Speciation has led to a wide dispersion of lifestyles. Some species demand highly oxygenated, cool mountain streams; others require stagnant, poorly oxygenated pools that may even evaporate at certain times of the year; still others live in tidal estuaries with daily fluctuations in salinity; and some benthic species live in the depths of the ocean still to be explored by man. Between all these is a complete range of environments, virtually all supporting piscine life. This diversification of habitats has led to differing physiological development to meet the requirements of the fish contained in them.

THE FISH'S ENVIRONMENT

In attempting to understand the form and function of fish, it is necessary first to understand the medium, water, in which they exist. Water is some 800 times denser than the air in which we terrestrial creatures live. Think of the effort we exert in swimming one length of the swimming pool, then consider that this effort is required all the time by fish.

The lifestyle of a fish can often be determined by looking at the shape of the body and fins, even though you may never before have come across the particular species. Much of the experienced aquarist's intuition is based on nothing more than a visual analysis of the fish in question. In the interests of efficiency, fish body forms have evolved to function with the minimum of fuel, which derives from the nutrients extracted from feeding. Fish from fast-flowing waters and those that spend much of their time in the middle and upper layers of water (pelagic species) tend to have a torpedo or fusiform body, which aids the flow of water over it.

If fish lead a sedentary life on the substrate, as do many catfish and loaches, for example, the body form differs. The underside is invariably flat, and the body is roughly triangular in cross-section. The paired fins (the pectoral and ventral fins) are broad and expanded to aid stability as the fish sits on the substrate and prevent it from being swept away by the current. In contrast, many surface-dwelling fish have flat or straight dorsal surfaces with upturned mouths, so that they can eat any nutrients that fall onto the surface of the water.

BODY PROTECTION

In many instances the body is covered partially or completely with scales, which are small, flexible plates embedded in the skin and arranged like overlapping tiles. In other species there are no scales; instead, the fish's body is protected by a covering of skin that is thicker than those with scales. Some fish are covered in bony plates, which, while looking superficially like thick scales, are, in fact, ossified bone which lacks the flexibility of scales. Fish with bony plates are often sedentary creatures because their body armor makes swimming for any distance difficult. The plates do, however, afford them protection, both from predators and from the environment.

FINS

The fins are usually membranes of skin, supported by skeletal bone. Although they appear similar, each fin performs a different function. There are generally three or four single, and one or two paired fins. Cichlids, with their slow deliberate movements, are ideal fish to observe in trying to understand the functions of these fins.

The single or unpaired fins on the back of the fish are the dorsal fins; the anal fin is on the underside behind the vent, and the caudal is the tail fin. The dorsal and anal fins are principally used to keep the fish upright when it is swimming. The caudal fin is the prime mover, equivalent to first gear in a car, and used to initiate forward movement. This movement is then maintained by sideways undulations of the body. Steering is aided by the ventral fins, and to a lesser extent by the pectoral fins, while the prime function of the pectoral fins is for low-speed maneuvering.

The shape of the fins will often indicate the fish's habits. Fins constitute drag in the water, yet are essential to movement. Pelagic fish from fast water or those that are constantly swimming generally have deeply forked caudal fins, and low or short dorsal and anal fins. Benthic, or bottom-dwelling, fish, which spend little of their time swimming, have a broad caudal fin with a heavy muscular base with which they can make quick dashes to safety when necessary.

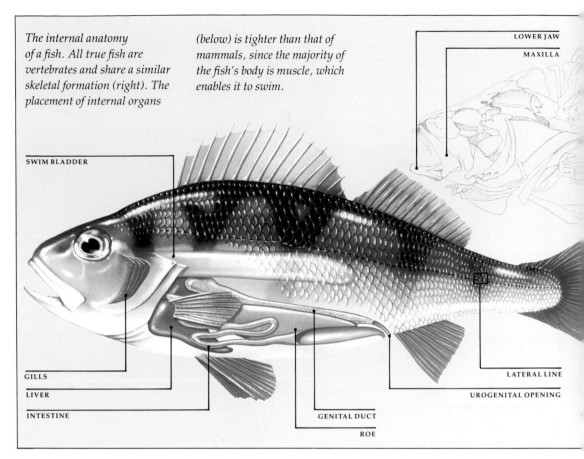

The internal anatomy of a fish. All true fish are vertebrates and share a similar skeletal formation (right). The placement of internal organs (below) is tighter than that of mammals, since the majority of the fish's body is muscle, which enables it to swim.

LOWER JAW
MAXILLA
SWIM BLADDER
GILLS
LIVER
INTESTINE
GENITAL DUCT
ROE
LATERAL LINE
UROGENITAL OPENING

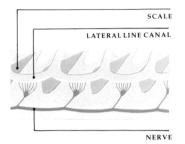

SCALE
LATERAL LINE CANAL
NERVE

ABOVE *A vertical section through the lateral line. This unique sensory organ, clearly visible on many species, detects variations in water pressure around the fish.*

THE SWIM BLADDER AND BUOYANCY

A fish's position in the water column is largely determined by its buoyancy. Some parts of a fish, such as the skeleton and certain visceral organs, are heavier than water, and others, such as fatty tissues and the swim bladder, which gives the fish buoyancy or lift, are lighter than water with a lower specific gravity. The swim bladder is an important controlling element. It is principally a gas-filled bladder, situated just below the vertebrae and extending from behind the head back for about one-third of the length of the fish, although this varies from species to species – some bottom-dwelling fish, which do not require the buoyancy, have a greatly reduced swim bladder, for example.

In most cases, the negative and positive buoyancy forces are directly in line and opposed. However, in some species this is not the case, with the result that when a fish is stationary in mid-water it lies at a slight angle, either head up, as the Pencilfish and Glass Catfish, or head down, as the Headstanding Characin.

RESPIRATION

The constant opening and closing of the mouth is central to the fish's method of respiration. Fish do not breathe atmospheric air; there are some exceptions, but in these cases it is supplementary to the principal method described here. Instead of lungs, fish have gills, filamentous organs that are located on each side at the back of the mouth, just in front of the throat. Water is pumped over the gills, which are richly supplied with blood vessels very near the surface. It is here that the dissolved oxygen in the water is absorbed into the blood stream and the waste gases are exchanged. The opening and closing of the mouth serves to pump new water into the mouth and over the gills and return it to the outside via the gill slits, which may be seen from the outside of the fish at the back of the head on each side.

The consumption of oxygen will vary according to the differing metabolic rates of each species and its immediate activity. Because water is so dense, respiration requires an abundance of energy, yet despite this fish are extremely efficient at converting the dissolved oxygen.

To protect the delicate gill filaments from damage from food particles or sand taken into the mouth during feeding, the bony arches to which the gills are attached have comb-like teeth to trap debris and deflect it away from the gills.

Fish have nostrils, although these are not used for respiration. Their sole use is as an olfactory or smell organ. Most fish have two pairs of nostrils, although some have only one pair. Inside the nostril is a series of lung-like rosettes, over which the water being sampled is passed.

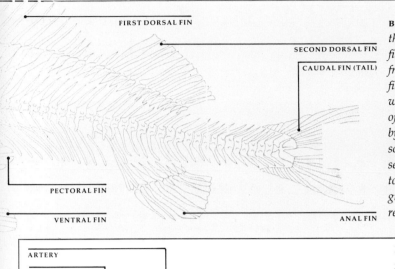

FIRST DORSAL FIN

SECOND DORSAL FIN

CAUDAL FIN (TAIL)

PECTORAL FIN

VENTRAL FIN

ANAL FIN

BELOW *A vertical section through the gill filaments of a fish. The gills extract oxygen from the water to oxygenate the fish's blood and also remove waste carbon dioxide. The rows of delicate filaments are protected by a thin covering. Although some fish have evolved secondary systems to enable them to breathe atmospheric air, the gills remain the primary respiratory organ.*

ABOVE *The fish's scales overlap to form a flexible "armor" that streamlines and protects the body.*

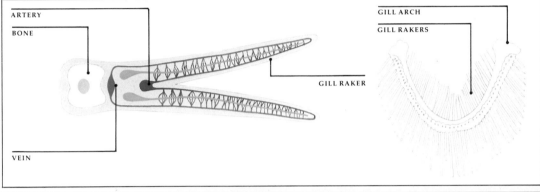

ARTERY

BONE

GILL ARCH

GILL RAKERS

GILL RAKER

VEIN

TASTE

Taste can be differentiated from smell in that taste is a result of intimate contact while smell is remote. Fish have no central organ for taste. Instead taste receptors are scattered over the surface of the head and body. In some species, such as catfish, the taste organs are also liberally spread over the barbels surrounding their mouth, acting much in the manner of an external tongue. Taste and smell are the prime senses required in finding food.

VISION

The eyes of fish are not unlike our own, but they are modified for focus to counter the refractive index of water. There is a species from South America, *Anableps anableps*, the so-called Four-eyed Fish, that has an eye with what can be best described as bifocal vision, allowing the fish to focus both below and above the water surface.

Fish lack eyelids, the eye being cleaned by the water. The eyes are usually positioned on the side of the head, giving virtually all-round vision although not a stereoscopic image. There are, however, some instances of binocular vision, particularly with some predators such as the pike.

Many bottom-dwelling fish have eyes toward the top of their head, although fish living in these environments, in which water turbulence tends to cloud the water, often depend more on smell and taste than on sight. As a result, the eye is greatly reduced in size. When bottom-dwellers are found in shallow areas, the retina of the dorsally placed eyes could be destroyed by strong sunlight penetrating the water, and in many of these cases the eye is protected by a flap of skin. Examples of this can be seen in some marine stingrays and freshwater loricariid catfish.

Careful analysis of a fish's physique and behavior will often give good indication as to its lifestyle, which must be emulated in the captive conditions of the aquarium. One of the easiest and most pleasant tasks for a fishkeeper is to observe the fish in the aquarium; far better still is to analyze just what is occurring and for what reason. Most behavioral discoveries have been recorded not by scientists, but by dedicated aquarists.

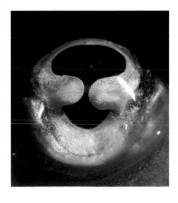

LEFT *It's easy to see how the Four-eyed Fish got its name. The eye is divided into two sections to allow for the differing refractive indices of air and water: the upper half allows* Anableps *clear vision above water while the lower lets it see prey, or predators, below water.*

FROM FISH FARM TO AQUARIUM

In the early days of fishkeeping, the only fish available to aquarists were those caught in the wild. They endured long journeys by sea in earthenware pots, and those who transported them had no idea of their needs or even cared about their welfare. Fortunately things have improved.

Many tropical freshwater fish are now bred commercially, and fish farming is an important part of the economy in countries such as Singapore, Thailand and Hong Kong. In the United States, too, the fish farms of Florida are noted for the quality of fish they provide for the trade. More recently, the Czech Republic has become an important source of captive-bred fish, especially for the European market.

Although fish farming is important from the conservationist point of view because it does not deplete wild stocks, it can be successful in the long term only if the occasional wild-caught fish is introduced to the breeding stock to improve the genetic base. In Singapore, work has been carried out on line breeding for the maintenance of healthy, viable stock as well as for "improvement" to finnage and body shape. Without careful line breeding, the stock would degenerate into small, weak fish with no marketable value.

ABOVE *Fish are brought together from various specialist breeders and held in large holding vats or tanks prior to shipping.*

RIGHT *As they may be in transit for many hours, the fish are packed in plastic bags with the minimum amount of water and maximum amount of air, oxygen, or air/oxygen mix.*

BOTTOM RIGHT *It is of great importance to make sure that you are buying healthy fish. Reputable establishments will always advise and make sure that the fish are caught and bagged efficiently, thus reducing the amount of stress on the creatures.*

TRANSPORTING FISH

Fish from the farms are packed for transportation with a small amount of water and, for most species, the remainder of the bag is filled with oxygen or an air/oxygen mix so that there is enough to keep the largest possible number of fish alive and well in the minimum volume of water during transit; oxygen is not normally used for anabantids or other air-breathing fish, as it can damage the fish. Sometimes tranquilizers are used in order to sedate particularly active or large fish and thus slow down their metabolism and hence reduce the amount of oxygen they will use during the journey. Transit time from fish farm to importer can be up to 36 hours, although with modern long-haul jets and careful timing of shipments, every effort is made to guarantee that the fish are in transit for the shortest possible time.

Wild-caught fish are also shipped in. These are collected from the rivers, streams and lakes, and taken to a holding station before being shipped out in a similar manner to farmed fish. The problem with these is that they require more expertise on the part of the importer in the provision of correct facilities to guarantee a good survival rate.

Marine fish have to endure the same rigors of transportation as freshwater species. Fewer marine fish are captive bred, and most are wild caught. Marine fish are more often than not individually bagged for transportation, and, because fewer can be packed to a box, they command a proportionally higher price.

The ethics of importing wild-caught fish can be argued forever. Some countries, such as Brazil, Colombia and Peru, have imposed bans on collecting fish at certain times of the year so that fish have a chance to breed. A prime example of this is the Cardinal Tetra, *Paracheirodon axelrodi*, virtually all of which offered for sale are wild caught. It must be remembered, however, that the fish are collected at the end of the wet season when the rivers have receded, leaving cut-off lakes full of residual flood water which trap thousands of fish. These creatures would undoubtedly die by predation or desiccation as the waters evaporate, so the removal of these fish is doing little to deplete the wild populations.

Marine fish used to be caught using cyanide, but this practice is, naturally, frowned upon as it destroys life indiscriminately. Nowadays, divers use a variety of netting techniques to catch the fish, which are then placed individually into plastic bags. In this way only those species that are required are taken. By careful management, the reefs of the world can be cropped for the aquatic trade without harming the ecosystem.

Tropical fish come from some of the poorest regions of the world, and they provide a source of income for people who might otherwise have none. They are a multimillion dollar industry worldwide.

FILTRATION AND WATER QUALITY

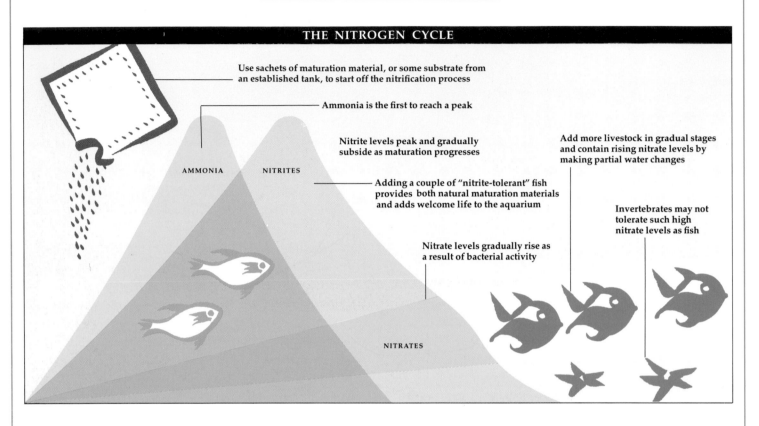

THE NITROGEN CYCLE

Use sachets of maturation material, or some substrate from an established tank, to start off the nitrification process

Ammonia is the first to reach a peak

Nitrite levels peak and gradually subside as maturation progresses

Add more livestock in gradual stages and contain rising nitrate levels by making partial water changes

AMMONIA   NITRITES

Adding a couple of "nitrite-tolerant" fish provides both natural maturation materials and adds welcome life to the aquarium

Invertebrates may not tolerate such high nitrate levels as fish

Nitrate levels gradually rise as a result of bacterial activity

NITRATES

The filtration system is the most important part of any aquarium, whether it is freshwater or marine. It is the fish's life-support system, and it must be considered at the outset so that you select the optimal system for the type of fish you are going to keep. Filtration systems can vary greatly in price, and a reputable dealer will be able to advise on one that is suitable for your aquarium and for your pocket.

THE NITROGEN CYCLE

In any body of water, the nitrogen cycle takes place. During this cycle, waste products from aquatic organisms, which are toxic to aquatic life, are converted into harmless nitrates, which are then absorbed by the plants. In the enclosed ecosystem of the aquarium, we have to allow for this cycle, and the filtration system is an integral part.

Fish produce waste and uneaten food decays in the aquarium. Ammonia and nitrites build up and these can be poisonous to fish. Ammonia-loving bacteria convert the ammonia into nitrite, then the nitrosomas, or nitrite-loving bacteria, convert the nitrites into harmless nitrates, which, in turn, are absorbed by the plants or removed during regular water changes. The efficiency of a filtration system is directly related to the surface area on which

the bacteria colonize to carry out their conversion and purification task.

When an aquarium is first set up, there will be very few bacteria, and they will not multiply until there is something for them to feed on. Initially, therefore, only a few fish should be added to the aquarium. The waste they produce will feed the bacteria, so the cycle begins. If you test the water regularly, you will find that at first there is no ammonia and no nitrite. As the wastes break down, the level of ammonia peaks; the bacteria feed, reproduce and reduce this level. Then there is a peak of nitrite, and the same reduction happens. After these two peaks the filtration system is said to "mature" – that is, it is able to support the number of fish in the aquarium. However, the introduction of more creatures means that the system once again goes through the peaks of ammonia and nitrite. As long as only a few fish are introduced each time, the system will cope. A problem will arise if too many fish are introduced at one time, and this should be avoided at all costs as it is the most common cause of death and disease.

Ammonia is highly toxic to fish. It converts easily to the less toxic ammonium, which can revert back to ammonia, and it is imperative to check ammonia levels at regular intervals in aquaria of hard, alkaline waters and marine waters. In acidic waters it is less of a problem.

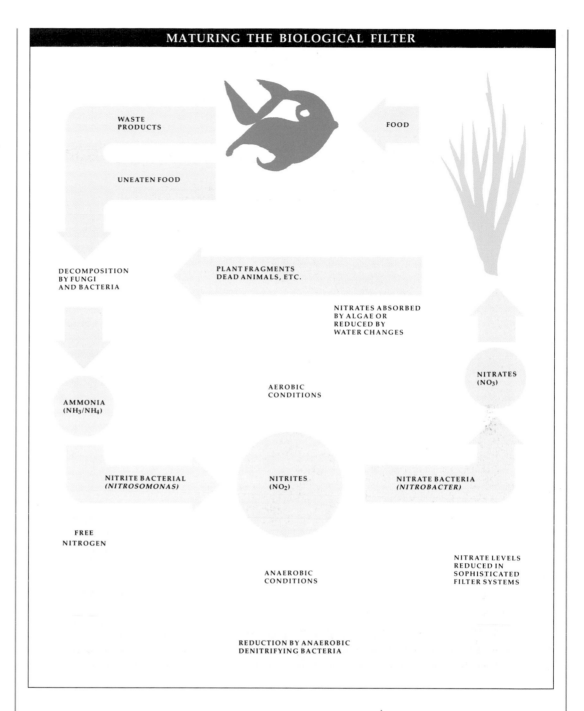

MATURING THE BIOLOGICAL FILTER

WASTE
PRODUCTS

FOOD

UNEATEN FOOD

DECOMPOSITION
BY FUNGI
AND BACTERIA

PLANT FRAGMENTS
DEAD ANIMALS, ETC.

NITRATES ABSORBED
BY ALGAE OR
REDUCED BY
WATER CHANGES

NITRATES
(NO₃)

AEROBIC
CONDITIONS

AMMONIA
(NH₃/NH₄)

NITRITE BACTERIAL
(NITROSOMONAS)

NITRITES
(NO₂)

NITRATE BACTERIA
(NITROBACTER)

FREE
NITROGEN

NITRATE LEVELS
REDUCED IN
SOPHISTICATED
FILTER SYSTEMS

ANAEROBIC
CONDITIONS

REDUCTION BY ANAEROBIC
DENITRIFYING BACTERIA

RIGHT *Establishing a well-balanced nitrogen cycle is crucial. The waste matter from plants and fish decomposes and forms ammonia. Bacteria in the water convert the ammonia into nitrites, which are, in turn, converted into nitrates, which are taken up by the plants.*

New-tank syndrome is widely recognized. The fish appear healthy and active when they are first placed in the tank, but after a couple of days, as the ammonia levels build, the fish become lethargic and may hang at the surface. If the fish survive this, they will go through a similar experience when the nitrites peak. The temptation is to break down the tank and start again or to do a massive water change. Neither of these will solve the problem and deaths will occur. The aquarium has to go through these natural cycles, and changing the water is just setting the process back a stage by removing any bacteria that have already started to multiply. Patience is the key to success.

It is possible to shorten the time needed for the build up of bacteria by using a commercial culture or by seeding the tank with gravel or filter medium from an existing, mature system.

FILTRATION SYSTEMS

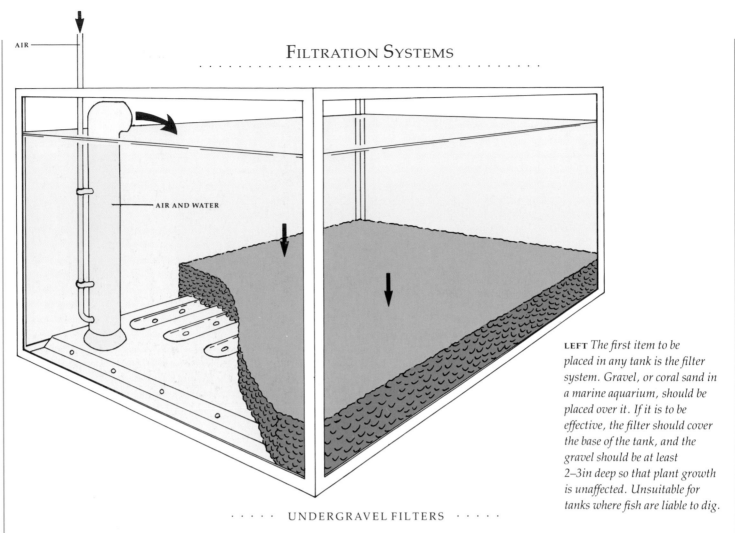

AIR

AIR AND WATER

LEFT *The first item to be placed in any tank is the filter system. Gravel, or coral sand in a marine aquarium, should be placed over it. If it is to be effective, the filter should cover the base of the tank, and the gravel should be at least 2–3in deep so that plant growth is unaffected. Unsuitable for tanks where fish are liable to dig.*

· · · · · UNDERGRAVEL FILTERS · · · · ·

These are perforated plates placed on the base of the aquarium with the substrate spread on top. Water is drawn down through the gravel and returned via the uplift (see diagram). The gravel or sand substrate acts as a filter bed, the bacteria building up within it and breaking down the waste products. The flow of water provides the oxygen that the bacteria require to live. This type of filtration system should not be switched off, because the aerobic bacteria will die if they are deprived of oxygen and be replaced by anaerobic species, which will quickly pollute the aquarium.

· · · · · REVERSE-FLOW · · · · ·
UNDERGRAVEL FILTERS

These are installed in same way as the standard undergravel system, but they operate in reverse (see diagram). Instead of the water being drawn down through the gravel, it is taken in by the pump and returned by forcing it up through the gravel.

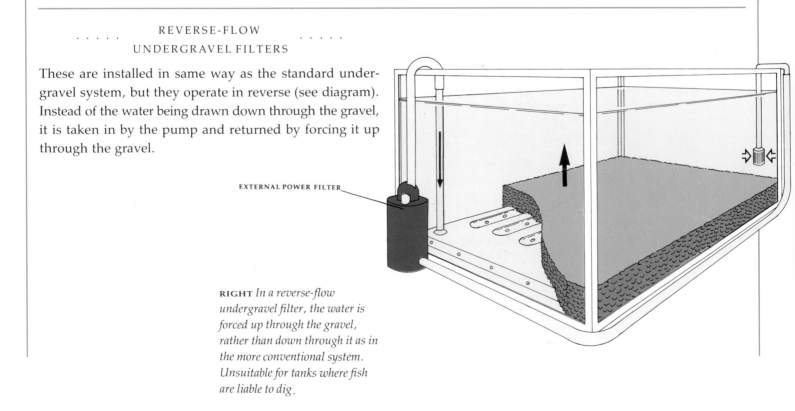

EXTERNAL POWER FILTER

RIGHT *In a reverse-flow undergravel filter, the water is forced up through the gravel, rather than down through it as in the more conventional system. Unsuitable for tanks where fish are liable to dig.*

· · · · · INTERNAL BOX FILTERS · · · · ·

Although they are not really suitable for community aquaria, internal box filters are often used in breeding tanks. They are simple to operate, air being used to draw the water through the filter medium (see diagram). How- ever, because they are small, they are of only limited effectiveness. As with undergravel filters, the water movement through the filter should not be interrupted or the bacterial colony will break down.

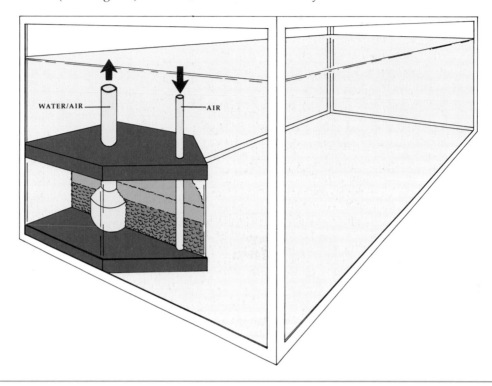

RIGHT *Internal box filters need only have an air supply connected for the water to be drawn through the filter medium. These simple filters are ideal for breeding tanks, but they are not convenient in fully furnished aquaria when they are difficult to get to for maintenance.*

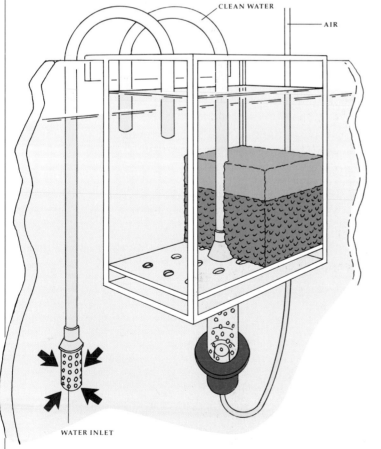

· · · · · EXTERNAL BOX FILTERS · · · · ·

These filters are not as common as they once were. They are air operated or are provided with a small electric pump (see diagrams), and they have the disadvantage of having to be clipped to the outside of the aquarium. Most modern tanks are not designed for this, and even the hoods have to be modified by cutting out various parts to accommodate this system.

LEFT *External box filters are rarely seen these days as tanks are not designed to accommodate them. They are operated by air from a small, electric pump which is situated to the side of the aquarium. The main disadvantage is that the hood or cover on the aquarium will need to be cut to accommodate the tubes.*

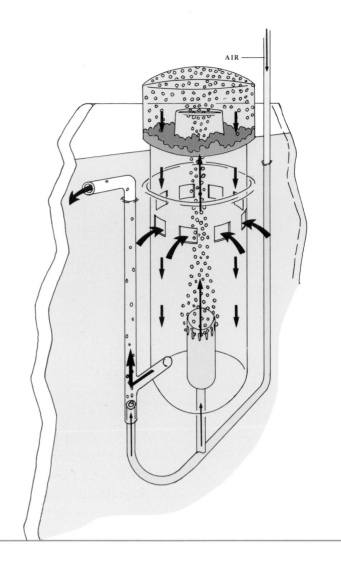

· · · · · PROTEIN SKIMMERS · · · · ·

Although they are not strictly filters, these devices are used in marine systems to provide aeration and to collect excess wastes such as proteins, hence the name. They are essential in the marine aquarium if any degree of long-term success is to be achieved.

In a vigorously aerated enclosed column of water, the harmful waste products attach themselves to the tiny air bubbles, which are transported to the top of the column and appear as a froth which spills over into the collecting chamber where the bubbles burst and the resulting murky brown residue can be discarded (see diagram). Several versions are available, ranging from air-operated models to more powerful and efficient motorized versions.

RIGHT *Protein skimmers are used to collect organic waste in marine aquaria, and they are essential pieces of equipment. Foam is produced by the energetic aeration action, and waste protein and other organic matter is carried in the foam and trapped in a collection chamber, which can be emptied periodically.*

AIR

CLEAN WATER

ADVISABLE TO FIT STRAINER BASKET TO INLET TO PREVENT SUCKING IN SMALL FISH — **WATER INLET**

· · · · · INTERNAL POWER FILTERS · · · · ·

The power source for these is a sealed electric motorized pump. Check carefully in the instructions to make sure that the unit is correctly installed. Some models can be completely submerged, while others should be placed with the outflow at the surface. The diagram shows how this type of filter works. The bacteria bed forms on the filter media, usually an open cell foam, which has a large surface area.

Internal power filters come in a variety of sizes to suit most small to medium-sized aquaria. They are also extremely useful when used as additional systems in larger aquaria to introduce water movement to stagnant areas of the tank.

LEFT *The element of an internal water filter is immersed in the water of the aquarium, and the return tube is at water level.*

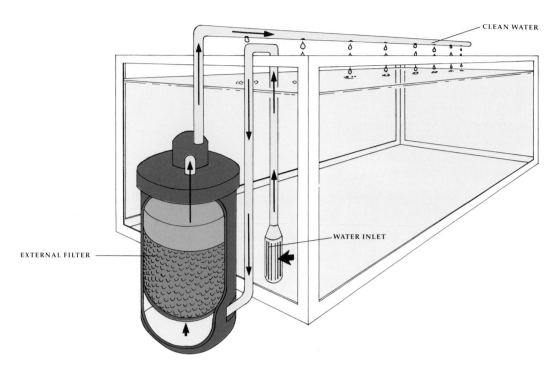

EXTERNAL FILTER

CLEAN WATER

WATER INLET

· · · · · EXTERNAL POWER FILTERS · · · · ·

ABOVE *The water pump of an external water filter is mounted on top of the canister.*

These are canisters with an electrical motor on top. The canister is filled with filtration media, and water flows into the canister from the aquarium and is pumped back (see diagram). As with the internal power filters, these come in a variety of sizes to suit the largest aquaria.

· · · · · EXTERNAL BIOLOGICAL SYSTEMS · · · · ·

These are probably some of the most efficient systems, but they are not readily available. As can be seen in the diagram, water is circulated through a series of compartments, each filled with filtration media. The composition of the medium will depend on the type of fish being kept. The water overflows from the aquarium into the filtration tank, and a submersible pump returns it to the aquarium.

The advantages of this system are manifold, the most obvious being the increased volume of water and surface area available for oxygen/carbon dioxide exchange. The second tank also provides a place to hide heaters and thermostats, thus leaving the show tank free of unsightly wires, while the submersible pump helps to heat the water. A disadvantage is the cost because you are, in effect, buying two aquaria, but this is probably outweighed by the benefits the system offers your fish.

LEFT *External biological filter systems are efficient but, unfortunately, not widely available. They work on the basis of filtering water through a series of compartments, each of which is filled with a filtration medium.*

ANTI-SIPHON HOLE

WATER FLOWS BY GRAVITY FROM MAIN AQUARIUM

GLASS DIVIDERS

FILTER WOOL

PERFORATED PLATE ON RUNNERS

COARSE FILTER SAND

MEDIUM FILTER SAND

FINE FILTER SAND

ELECTRIC PUMP RETURNS WATER TO THE AQUARIUM

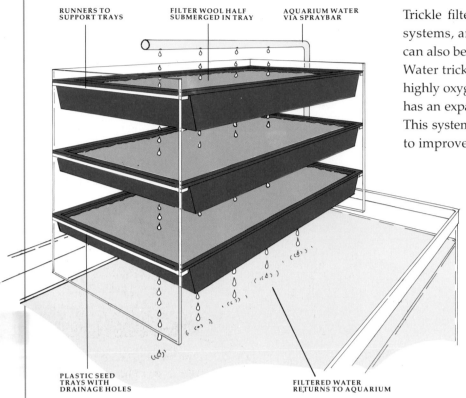

RUNNERS TO
SUPPORT TRAYS

FILTER WOOL HALF
SUBMERGED IN TRAY

AQUARIUM WATER
VIA SPRAYBAR

PLASTIC SEED
TRAYS WITH
DRAINAGE HOLES

FILTERED WATER
RETURNS TO AQUARIUM

· · · · · TRICKLE FILTERS · · · · ·

Trickle filters, which are sometimes also called wet/dry systems, are often used in marine systems, although they can also be used to great advantage in freshwater aquaria. Water trickles through a series of filter beds and becomes highly oxygenated in the process because the filter medium has an expansive area directly exposed to air (see diagram). This system is often coupled with one of the other systems to improve a filtration system.

LEFT *Trickle filters are excellent supplementary filtration systems. As the filter beds are partially exposed to air, there is a greater area for oxygen exchange and they can therefore support a large number of nitrifying bacteria.*

WATER MAINTENANCE
· ·

No matter how good the filtration system is, it will not dispense with the need for regular water changes. In the closed system of the aquarium, toxins can build up quickly and sometimes with devastating effects, but you can reduce the chance of this happening by careful maintenance of the aquarium and regular monitoring of water quality.

Every 7–10 days carry out a partial water change. Remove 10–15 percent of the water and at the same time siphon out any fish feces, decaying plant material and uneaten, decomposing food. The replacement water should be of similar temperature. The main problem with tap water is that it contains chlorine added by the water company to make it fit for human consumption. To make it acceptable for fish, either leave it to stand for 24 hours to disperse the chlorine naturally or add a dechlorinator, which has the effect of neutralizing the chlorine within seconds, thus rendering it fit for fish.

WATER CHEMISTRY
· ·

The degree acidity or alkalinity of water is referred to as pH. The pH range is from 0 (very acid) to 14 (very alkaline), with 7, the mid-point, being referred to as neutral. The pH scale is logarithmic, and therefore a change of one unit represents a 10-fold change – pH 8 is 10 times more alkaline than pH 7, and pH 9 is 100 times more alkaline than pH7. In terms of the acidity values, pH 6 is 10 times more acidic than pH 7, and pH 5, is 100 times more acidic than pH 7. The appropriate pH level for every freshwater fish is given in the second part of this book.

Water hardness is another area that can cause concern. The hardness is graded by the amount of dissolved salts in the water, and the most often used scales in fishkeeping are °dH and mg/litre of calcium carbonate ($CaCO_3$). Very soft water would be in the region of 3°dH or 0–50mg/l $CaCO_3$) and very hard 25°dH (in excess of 450mg/l $CaCO_3$).

Most fish have a wide tolerance of pH and water hardness. They will adapt to a pH range between 6.5 and 8.5 and to a water hardness of 9–14°dH. However, some fish have specific requirements, and unless you are willing to provide them, any attempt at keeping them will be doomed to failure from the outset. These are often wild-caught fish. Farm-raised specimens will tolerate a wide range of water conditions, but wild-caught fish are very precise in their requirements so do check on whether you are purchasing wild or farmed specimens.

HEATING
AND LIGHTING

To the uninitiated the very words "tropical fish" evoke an image of large fuel bills and complex heating systems. This may have been true in the past, but modern heating units are easy to install, safe to use, and economical to maintain.

HEATING

Heater/thermostats may be purchased as a combined unit. They come in various wattages and are pre-set to about 72°F. They may be adjusted by turning the knob that protrudes from the top. Check the manufacturer's instructions to see whether these should be totally or partially submerged. Alternatively, a separate submersible heater, an undertank heating mat, or a heating cable and external thermostat may be used. Some brands of external power filters also have integral heating units, and these are another means of warming the aquarium water. After connecting the heating equipment to the power supply, **never** switch on a submersible heater unless it is below water.

As a general guide, allow about 10 watts of heating per 1 gallon of aquarium water. Thus a tank measuring 24 × 12 × 12in and containing approximately 12 gallons of water would require a 125w heater.

LIGHTING

Lighting is a matter for individual taste. The most popular method of illuminating the aquarium is by using fluorescent lights. These are available in a wide variety of spectral output, and the color produced may be biased toward the red end of the spectrum or to the blue. Red light penetrates water less easily than blue, and it is of greatest use to the human observer because it enhances the color of the fish. You can obtain specialized tubes that are designed to cover the spectral range for optimum plant growth, while others are designed not only to promote lush marine algal growth, but to provide the quality of light necessary for marine invertebrates to thrive.

Alternative lighting units are spotlights and metal halide lamps, which will penetrate the lower levels of deeper aquaria. These are used on open-topped tanks and the lighting is often supplemented with a fluorescent tube. Metal halide lamps plus an actinic blue tube are particularly effective on marine aquaria in which invertebrates are kept.

The amount of lighting required will depend on what

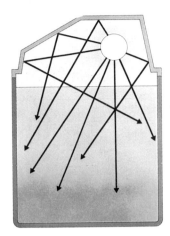
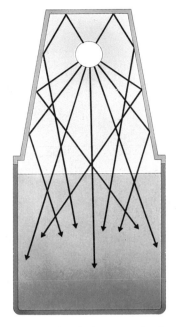
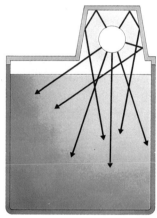

ABOVE *The ideal position for the light is directly above the tank.*

BELOW LEFT *If a small reflector is placed towards the front, the back of the tank is left in shadow.*

TOP LEFT *Lights towards the front of the tank and a medium-sized reflector give good all-round illumination.*

you are trying to achieve. A fully planted freshwater aquarium needs the intense lighting to simulate tropical sunlight. To achieve this three, or even four, fluorescent tubes will be needed, and these should be controlled with a timer so that they come on in sequence and go off in sequence over a period of 12 hours (tropical day length), with a peak of six hours when all tubes are on to give the intensity of light the tropical water plants require for growth. However, if you have decided to decorate your aquarium with plastic plants or maybe with no plants at all, you will only need sufficient light to observe your fish by.

In marine aquaria where there are corals, anemones and the like, the need for intense lighting is paramount. However, for fish alone the lighting is of less importance, and you will need only enough light to allow you to observe the fish. This has the advantage of reducing the amount of green algae that will occur, but the disadvantage of encouraging the growth of brown, red or black algae, especially if water conditions begin to deteriorate, because they flourish in lower light levels.

THE FRESHWATER AQUARIUM

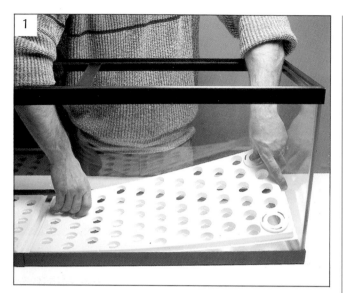

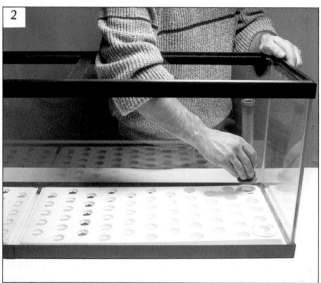

Having purchased a tank, stand and ancillary equipment from your dealer, you now have the task of setting everything up. Make sure that the site you have chosen will take the weight of the aquarium when it is fully set up. Although water is clear, it is heavy – 1 gallon weighs approximately 10 pounds – add this to the gravel, rocks, tank and stand, and you will understand why the floor needs to be capable of withstanding a considerable load.

Place the stand in position and check that it is level. If you have an all-glass aquarium, place some styrofoam tiles on top of the stand before positioning the aquarium. The tiles will absorb any minor irregularities, which might otherwise place stress on the aquarium and cause it to fracture. Rinse out the aquarium with plain water (do not use soap), then fill it to check for leaks. This may seem like a waste of time, but accidents do happen. There may be a fault in the manufacture, or the tank may have been damaged in transit. It is easier and quicker to empty, dry and reseal a tank at this stage than to have to remove substrate, plants and equipment first.

If you are using undergravel filtration, attach the uplift tubes and air line (if it is to be air-operated) or power heads, and place the filter plates on the base glass. Seat your rocks and wood if you are including it on the filter bed. This will stop the fish from undermining them with the result that they may topple against the tank glass and crack it. Next cover the filter plate with well-washed gravel. If you are not using an undergravel system, seat the rocks and wood on the base glass for the same reasons.

LEFT *Setting up the tank*

1 *The baseplate of a biological or subgravel filter is placed in the bottom of the tank.*
2 *The bubble airlift is located in the rear corner of the filter plate.*
3 *The plate is covered with gravel, to a depth of at least 3in.*
4 *A submerged heater with a thermostat is placed in the tank. Before being switched on, the heater should be raised to about 2in above the gravel. It can be attached to the side of the tank with rubber suckers.*
5 *Fitting the air pump to the bubble airlift. It is advisable to secure any trailing wires to avoid accidental disconnection.*
6 *Decorating the tank: waterworn wood, if well soaked in advance to remove any impurities, and aquatic plants make attractive additions.*

HEATING AND LIGHTING

The heating system and the lighting system can be connected together, but do not, at this time, plug them into the electric supply. Follow the manufacturer's instructions. Use a cord reel to avoid having too many trailing cables. This allows all the electrical equipment – heater/thermostats, filters, air pumps, and lights – to be wired into a single unit so that you have only a single cable going to the plug. Heater/thermostats are supplied with suckers so that you can attach them to the aquarium glass. Place the unit according to the manufacturer's instructions. Some units are totally submersible and need to be positioned at an angle, with the thermostat higher than the heater element; other kinds must be vertical with the very top part above the water surface. For safety, check it first – electricity and water do not mix! Never cover this form of heating unit with gravel.

FILLING THE TANK

The aquarium may now be filled with water. Place a piece of brown wrapping paper, an upturned saucer, or a similar object on the gravel and pour the water onto this to avoid disturbing the substrate. Fill the tank to above the level of the heating units, but it is best not to fill the aquarium completely yet as you still have to plant the plants, and it is easier to work in a three-quarters full tank than to have to mop up all the water spilt from working in a full aquarium.

Check that everything is connected together properly. If necessary, attach the air line from the undergravel filter to the air pump and make sure that you have included a non-return valve in the line (this is especially important if you cannot position the air pump above the aquarium) to prevent any back siphoning. Shorten any over-long cords. You may now connect it to the electricity supply. Allow the tank to settle for 24 hours, during which time you can check that the heater is set at the right temperature and make any adjustments. Use a thermometer to check the temperature variance. There will be a diurnal fluctuation of several degrees, but do not be worried by this. It is a phenomenon that occurs in nature and, because the change in either direction is gradual, the fish and plants can adjust to it. There are several different types of thermometer available; some go in the tank, others are stuck on the outside. If you use an external type, remember that it can be affected by other heat sources, so make sure that it is not positioned where sunlight can fall on it, or next to a radiator or lamp.

LEFT *Plants also contribute to water filtration and quality, but require assistance from other filters.*

PLANTING AND DECORATION

Decorating the aquarium is a matter of personal taste. If you are using plastic plants, these can be put into position before the aquarium is filled with water, but if you use real ones, it is better to plant them in warm water and not shock them by placing them in cold water.

When choosing the plants, make sure that they are suitable for aquatic use. Terrestrial plants, such as *Fittonia, Hypoestes, Spathiphyllum, Caladium, Dieffenbachia, Maranta* and *Pilea*, are increasingly offered as aquarium plants. Some will survive for perhaps as little as four weeks underwater whereas true aquatic plants will thrive. Plan your planting scheme before starting and you can ascertain the type and number of plants you will require.

For the beginner some of the best plants are the various species of *Cryptocoryne, Echinodorus, Ludwigia, Hygrophila, Aponogeton* and *Bacopa*. Although the fine-leaved *Cabomba* is very attractive, it can be difficult to grow, so it is wise to leave this until you are a little more experienced. When you plant them, remember what you do with garden plants and space them out and plant them individually. The planting distance will be the spread of the leaves, and the rows of each species should be staggered so that when they are seen from the front you see a wall of plants but when they are viewed from above, each plant has its own space and light can penetrate to the lower leaves. Although this technique takes time and patience, it does prevent the plants from being damaged when planting. Remember, too, that these are tropical plants, which require quite intense light, and if the lower leaves are deprived of this they will die and decay.

Top up the tank and leave it to run for several days to settle the plants and allow the filter beds to begin to work. When you add the fish, do so a few at a time (see filtration section and new tank syndrome). Time and patience are the keys to success.

CHOOSING FISH

ABOVE *Once the system has matured, it will have a full complement of fish and the plants will be flourishing.*

The choice of fish is up to you, but be guided by a reputable retailer if you are unsure. Always look to see that the fish are healthy and are not swimming around with their fins clamped or just hanging in the water. This means a little research before you go to the store so that you can be sure that the fish are behaving as they are supposed to – for example, *Corydoras* should be grubbing around on the bottom, while *Danios* will be swimming in a school. The fish will be caught and put into a plastic bag, which is sealed and placed in a darker bag to keep the fish quiet during transit. When you arrive home, float the plastic bag in the aquarium for an hour or so to allow the water temperatures to equalize. Then the fish may be released.

Most people like to quarantine their fish before adding them to their main tank. This requires a separate aquarium. If you are unable to do this, then it is doubly important that you only buy quality, compatible stock from a reputable dealer. Never buy on impulse.

TEMPERATURE CONVERSION

°C	°F
[1] 100	212
95	203
90	194
85	185
80	176
75	167
70	158
65	149
60	140
55	131
50	122
45	113
40	104
35	95
30	86
[2] 25	77
20	68
15	59
10	50
5	41
[3] 0	32

[1] *Water boils*
[2] *Normal tank temperature for tropical fish is between 20–25°C/68–77°F*
[3] *Water freezes*

Five Centigrade degrees are equal to nine Fahrenheit degrees. Simple formulae for conversion are:

$$((°C \times 9) \div 5) + 32 = °F$$

$$((°F - 32) \times 5) \div 9 = °C$$

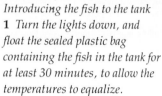

Introducing the fish to the tank
1 *Turn the lights down, and float the sealed plastic bag containing the fish in the tank for at least 30 minutes, to allow the temperatures to equalize.*
2 *Open the plastic bag, and, with gentle scooping movements, introduce the tank water to it. Give the fish plenty of time to adjust.*
3 *Tip over the bag to release the fish into the tank. It may take several days for the fish to adjust properly to its new environment.*

The only other items you will need are nets for catching the fish, an algae magnet or similar for cleaning the inside of the front glass, a siphon tube for water changes, and buckets for transporting water. It is also wise to keep spares for air pumps and power filters as well as having a spare heater/thermostat, and you will need supplies of filter media if you are using a type that requires filter wool and carbon.

BELOW *A well-planted aquarium makes a wonderful focal point in any room. Careful planning in the first instance is essential in order to achieve the finished product.*

THE MARINE AQUARIUM

The main factors in setting up a marine aquarium are fairly similar to those for freshwater, and you should read the sections on setting up a freshwater tank and on filtration. One vital point is that neither the tank nor any other fittings in contact with the marine water should be metallic; if they are, toxins may develop that could harm the fish or the invertebrates – such as sea anemones, fan worms, shrimp and other crustacea, molluscs, and echinoderms. This consideration extends to the containers used to mix the marine salt or to store replacement water as well as such accessories as nets with metallic handles. These days all-glass tanks held together by silicone sealant are usual, and they are ideal for this purpose. Not many years ago, however, tanks, particularly large ones, had metal frames and, unless these were of stainless steel, were unsuitable for marine use.

Another general rule is to start with the largest tank you can accommodate. The reason is that water conditions are more stable and easier to control in a large body of water, whereas they can become unstable very rapidly in a small marine tank. Also remember, that stocking levels in a marine aquarium are much lower than can be tolerated in a freshwater aquarium – only half the number of fish can be maintained compared to a freshwater system.

ABOVE *Although a little more difficult than a freshwater set-up, the rewards of persevering with a marine system can be spectacular.*

OPPOSITE *Careful selection of fish will ensure that you have a good balance in the aquarium. Be sure not to overstock or to choose fish which will bully their smaller companions.*

SALINITY

Inevitably the marine salt will be artificial. Do not use a local source of marine water, particularly from temperate areas, because the elevated temperature of a tropical marine culture can destroy existing bacteria and plankton, which is a recipe for disaster. Good brands of marine salt are expensive, but they do contain all the necessary trace elements.

Fortunately, marine waters have, for the most part, a pretty stable salinity and temperature level. The salinity level is a measure of the water's specific gravity. Pure freshwater has a specific gravity of 1.0; most marine water is in the range 1.023 to 1.027, although some bodies of marine water, such as the Red Sea, are a little higher. Specific gravity can be measured with a hydrometer, a standard piece of equipment for any marine aquarist. Some hydrometers also include a thermometer. Temperature, particularly for the commercially available species of fish, is fairly constant at 75–79°F.

Much of the water loss will be due to evaporation, particularly if the tank is uncovered to provide good light penetration, but also from any external biological filter, especially the trickle varieties. Only pure water evaporates, leaving the salts and trace elements to build up in the aquarium. This water should be replaced gradually by mature freshwater of a similar temperature. Always check afterward that the specific gravity of the new mix is as it should be. Only when water is removed should it be necessary to replace it with a marine mix.

The alkalinity, too, is pretty constant, at around 8.4 pH. However, never be complacent about water quality. It should always be regularly monitored, and you should pay particular attention to the nitrogen cycle – the conversion of ammonia created from waste material into nitrites, and subsequently into the more harmless nitrates. This conversion process is the prime function of the filtration system. Regardless of the filter, however, the ammonia levels must not be allowed to rise too high. Any increase in ammonia will lead to a proportional increase in nitrite and nitrates, both of which can have a dire consequence on the fish's health.

FILTERS

Most marine systems are equipped with biological filters, and some have supplementary mechanical filters to remove larger debris. These biological filters may take the form of sub-gravel, external or trickle systems, or even a combination of two or more elements. As with freshwater systems, you should think about and plan the filtration system well in advance, for it will pay dividends in the long term. The importance of the efficiency of the filtration system, particularly with marine installations, cannot be overemphasized.

Filters do not work efficiently from the moment they are first turned on. The bacteria that causes the chemical conversion of the nitrogen cycle take time to mature. This normally takes around 40 days and cannot be effectively shortened. During this period fish **must not** be added to the system. Initially, the ammonia level will increase, peaking after 8–10 days, it will then rapidly decrease to negligible levels. However, at this stage, the toxic nitrite levels see a proportional increase and will be at their highest at around 30 days into the filtration maturation period. After 40 days, the nitrite level diminishes, and the nitrate conversion should then be stable.

This maturation period assumes optimum conditions – that there have been no live introductions into the system and the filter has not been turned off. It is always advisable, particularly during initial set-up and maturity period, to constantly measure the chemical composition of the water using readily available test kits. Rises in harmful nitrite levels can just as easily occur with a mature system, and marine systems can fail alarmingly fast.

MARINE ENVIRONMENT

The level and type of lighting to be used will largely depend on whether or not invertebrates are to be included in the aquarium. Many invertebrates and some marine fish need algae in their diet, which high levels of lighting will promote. Some fish are unsuitable inmates with invertebrates – they will eat them – while other fish, such as the Percula Clowns, have a symbiotic relationship with anemones, both partners benefiting from the partnership.

High-intensity lighting can be achieved through the use of metal halide lamps, although these are expensive to both buy and run. Alternatively, fluorescent tubes can be used, mixing different color tubes to encompass the spectrum of normal sunlight that will encourage the development and growth of algae. It is advisable not to have cover glasses between the tank surface and the lights, as salt deposits soon build up on the glass.

If the aquarium is to include invertebrates, these should be introduced well in advance of the fish to allow them to settle. Invertebrates are generally more delicate and demanding than the fish and will require special attention. Even so, they should not be introduced until the filtration system has matured, and even then introduce them gradually. The same principal applies to the fish.

Most of the marine fish commercially available have been harvested from nature by professional divers and collectors. Unlike freshwater fish, few species are farmed or commercially bred. There are, of course, only finite numbers that can be extracted without damage to the natural ecosystem. Fortunately, at present demand seems comparatively low and their prices are correspondingly high. Although it is not the intention of the author to discourage the keeping of marine subjects, it is important to convey the complexity of keeping tropical marines. Experience with freshwater aquaria is advised before any attempt is made to keep marine fish. There are many publications specializing in the marine aquarium keeping, and those who wish to start in this part of the hobby should research fully beforehand.

Keeping a marine aquarium is both challenging and rewarding. Many of the fish have never before been spawned in captivity, and this represents the greatest challenge of all.

FEEDING

There are, on the market today, many kinds of commercially prepared foods for both freshwater and marine fish. Flakes, pellets, freeze-dried, frozen and live foods are all available, and the choice is yours. Before you decide what you think the fish will require, however, it is important that you determine what their natural diet is and what will form an effective substitute in captivity. Freshwater fish adapt comparatively readily to aquarium life, and many will take flake or tablet foods without any trouble. Marine fish can be a little more troublesome to feed, but most reputable retailers will be happy to tell you what the fish has been fed on and will advise on diet.

Fish can be carnivores (flesh eaters), omnivores (those with a varied diet), insectivores (fish that feed on adult or larval insects), herbivores (vegetarians), or piscivores (fish eating) and there are ranges of foods available to meet most of these needs. Flake foods will usually form the basic diet, but the introduction of frozen and live foods into the diet can greatly improve the quality of your fish. Carnivores, whose natural diet is live fish, can sometimes cause problems. Alternatives such as whole frozen lancefish or pieces of trout or coley are available, but these sometimes prove unacceptable and live fish are the only answer.

· · · · · FLAKE AND TABLET FOODS · · · · ·

These are commercially prepared and form the basis of a balanced diet for the average community of fish. Specialty flakes, for example, cichlids, marines, live-bearers and herbivores, are also available. These can be fed once a day. The quantity given will depend on the number of fish in the aquarium, but all the food should be consumed within 5–10 minutes; otherwise, it begins to decompose and foul the water.

· · · · · FROZEN FOODS · · · · ·

These are frozen and irradiated and are, therefore, disease free. They are a boon to marine keepers, as *Mysis* shrimp, krill, plankton and so on are all readily available in this form. For the freshwater enthusiast they are of equal value with brine shrimp, *Daphnia* and bloodworms among the most popular. Large foods, such as whole shrimp and lancefish, make a welcome addition to the diet of larger carnivores. When you feed this type of high protein or oily diet, make sure that you monitor the water conditions, because a build-up of proteins can quickly turn the water foul. Kept in the home freezer, small portions of frozen foods can be broken off as needed and fed to the fish.

· · · · · GREEN FOODS · · · · ·

Many herbivores cannot get sufficient nutrients from the algae in the aquarium, and a suitable substitute has to be found. The naturally produced algae should, if your system is properly established, be restricted in quantity, and the only natural alternatives are the soft-leaved plants. One of the easiest alternatives is lettuce, the outer leaves of which may be crushed in the hand and "planted" in the substrate or held down by a stone. Marine tangs are particularly partial to this, eagerly tearing at the leaf, and, among the freshwater fish, the loricariid catfishes will graze on the leaves until the leaves look like a piece of netting. Frozen peas may also be used; take the pea between the finger and thumb and squeeze it. Discard the seed coat and feed the soft, inner portion. Herbivores, unlike omnivores and, particularly, carnivores, require an abundance of green foods on which they will graze most of the day. However, lettuce and similar soft-leaved substitutes decay quickly in the warm conditions of the aquarium, so it is important to replace old leaves regularly, and this may mean feeding night and morning.

· · · · · LIVE FOODS · · · · ·

Perhaps the most natural way to feed your fish is with live foods, and these should, in the case of insectivores and omnivores, form a supplement to flake foods on a regular basis. *Daphnia*, midge and mosquito larvae occur worldwide and make excellent foods for freshwater species. *Daphnia*, or water fleas as they are more commonly known, are ideal for the small tetras and similar-sized fish, while larger fish, such as the Rainbows, will avidly

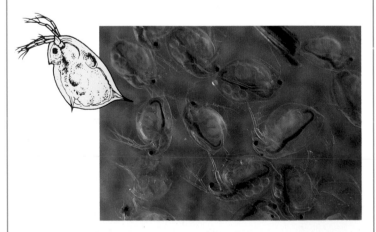

ABOVE *Water fleas, otherwise known as* Daphnia, *are available from most aquatic stores. They play an important part in the diet of many aquarium fish.*

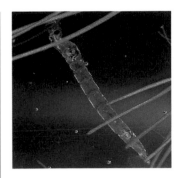

ABOVE *The transparent body of the glassworm makes it relatively easy to overlook. However, this creature can even be found under the ice in the depths of winter. Note the large jaws – do not feed it to young fish.*

ABOVE *Bloodworms are a useful food for helping to bring fish into breeding condition or for feeding bottom dwelling species.*

that you and your conscience have to come to terms with – do you feed live fish and keep your predator, or do you withhold the live fish in the hope that it will take dead foods, with the outcome that it may starve to death? It is often necessary in these cases to feed live fish until the predator is fully acclimatized to captive conditions, then it may be possible to wean them onto dead foods – but only in some cases. The decision is yours. Make it with care.

ABOVE *Always make sure that live* Tubifex *worms are well cleaned before feeding them to the fish. The worms feed by passing sludge through their bodies, and they need to be cleansed of this before being put into the aquarium.*

consume mosquito larvae. They are particularly useful for bringing fish into breeding condition. Not only are these nutritious, but they also give the fish its natural form of hunting and catching its own food. *Mysis* shrimp and brine shrimp are also available, and these may be used for both freshwater and marine subjects. For large carnivorous fish it is possible to purchase river shrimps, which are avidly consumed.

If your fish is a piscivore, the only thing you may be able to persuade it to eat is other fish. This is something

FISH HEALTH

Perhaps the single aspect that is most often overlooked in fish welfare is the effects of stress on fish. Obvious causes of stress are capture and transportation, and wholesalers recognize this and rest the fish before selling them on to retailers. Again, reputable retailers allow the stock a period of acclimatization before selling to the public. But some outlets are not so scrupulous, and the fish suffer as a result. Even in the aquarium fish suffer stress. Constant movement around the tank, bullying, harassment, the wrong water conditions or temperature range, a poorly maintained filtration system, and the resultant diminution of water quality – all these place unnecessary stress on the fish and leave the weakened creatures open to disease.

You are responsible for the lives of these creatures, and, as prevention is better than cure, you must always maintain the aquarium to the highest standards. Watch any new fish you add and check that the existing ones are not being bullied. Remember that some fish are active at night, so the bullying may be going on after dark. A couple of observational sessions at night, using a small red pygmy

lamp over the aquarium, should determine if this is the case. Once you have ascertained the problem, you can deal with it.

Although quarantining is always recommended and, for the most part, should be carried out in a bare aquarium, there are times when this is detrimental – with wild-caught, timid fish, for example. Experience has shown that quarantining in a fully mature system with well-aged water and an efficient filtration system combined with furnishings of live plants is beneficial for certain groups of fish – for example, the whiptail catfishes. These require algae in their diet and like to browse on plants or rest on wood. In a clinical, unfurnished tank, they become stressed and do not feed. On the other hand, fishes such as barbs, open-water, school fish, are quite happy being quarantined in clinical surroundings.

The subject of diseases is complex and we can only touch upon the subject here, listing some of the most common complaints. You should invest in a specialist fish health book if you intend taking the hobby further.

· · · · · WHITE SPOT · · · · ·

This is caused by the protozoa *Ichthyophthirius multifilis* in freshwater aquaria and *Cryptocaryon irritans* in marine aquaria. The first evidence of infection is a sprinkling of small white spots over the body and fins of the fish. As the fish become more infested, they dash around, scratching and flicking against objects in the aquarium. The parasite can be treated only during the free-swimming part of its lifecycle. Proprietary treatments are available for both freshwater and marine fish. Follow the instructions carefully. If there are invertebrates in the marine aquarium, check that the treatment used is not copper-based and toxic to marine invertebrates. Some freshwater fish, such as Clown Loaches, and some of the catfishes are sensitive to these treatments, which should be used at half-strength if these fish are present.

· · · · · VELVET · · · · ·

This is caused by Dinoflagellates, *Odinium* in freshwater fish and *Amyloodinium* in marines. The symptoms are a yellow-gray coating on the body, and the fish may scratch against rocks. You will also see rapid gill movements. This parasite is difficult to wipe out if it becomes established in the internal organs of the fish. For freshwater fish, treat *in situ* with a proprietary treatment. The treatment for marine fish is longer, lasting three to four weeks, and requires the use of a copper treatment.

· · · · · LARGER PARASITES · · · · ·

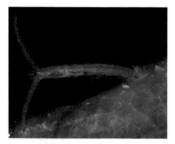

ABOVE *It is the female anchor worm that buries its head in the flesh of the fish.*

ABOVE *As the body of the fish louse (*Argulus*) is so transparent, this parasite is often overlooked. It can be introduced inadvertently if you are feeding live fish as food, so be sure to check before introducing them to the aquarium.*

Anchor worm (*Lernaea*) and fish lice (*Argulus*) are easily seen with the naked eye and are usually only found on newly imported freshwater fish. If you notice them in the dealer's stock, do not buy the fish, but if you do get them, they can easily be treated. Remove each *Lernaea* with a pair of tweezers. The head of the parasite embeds itself in the body of the fish, so grasp the parasite as close as possible to the fish and ease it away. Treat the wound with antiseptic. *Argulus*, which is disk-shaped, is more difficult to see because it has a transparent body. It clings to the body of the fish with suckers. The recognized treatment is with metriphonate, but care needs to be exercised because some fish, such as Piranhas, are sensitive to this.

· · · · · FUNGUS · · · · ·

RIGHT *Fungus is invariably a secondary infection. Any fish which may have been attacked by another fish or badly handled and has split fins, missing scales, cuts, etc., is open to attack by fungi.*

This usually occurs as a secondary infection after the fish has been attacked or mishandled or has cut itself. It resembles tufts of cotton on the fish. Treat as soon as possible with a proprietary substance. Fungal attacks seem rare on marine fish.

Unfertilized eggs are often affected by fungus. They should be removed before the infection spreads to the fertilized eggs. Some fungus remedies can also be used with fish eggs, but be sure to check with the manufacturer's instructions before you use them.

· · · · · FIN ROT · · · · ·

Fin rot has many causes, including poor water conditions, fin nipping and bad handling. It is a bacterial infection, which manifests itself in the early stages by the degeneration of the fin membrane and in later stages by the degeneration of the fin rays as well. There are several good and effective antibacterial remedies available. This is one infection that can be avoided by correct care and maintenance of the aquarium.

BREEDING STRATEGIES

LIVE-BEARERS

As their common name suggests, these fish give birth to live young. The eggs are fertilized inside the body of the female, where they develop in relative safety. Live-bearers produce relatively few young, but they are quite large and well developed when they are born. Although they will reproduce readily in a community aquarium, many of the fry will fall prey to other fishes. To avoid this, it is best to place the heavily gravid female in a separate tank with plenty of fine-leaved plants so that when the fry are born, they can hide from their mother, who will often eat her offspring. Breeding traps and nets are available, and these can be floated in the main aquarium and the female placed in them to give birth. They are effective for smaller live-bearers, but larger fish, such as swordtails and mollies, do not like being confined in such cramped conditions and will either try to jump out or, worse, die.

ABOVE *Even in a community aquarium, there is a quiet corner where Colisa chuna can build its bubble-nest and guard its eggs and fry. However, as the young become free-swimming, it is unlikely that many will survive as they will fall prey to other fish.*

EGG LAYERS

There are several categories of egg-laying fish.

· · · · · BUBBLE-NEST BUILDERS · · · · ·

The best known of the bubble-nest builders are the gouramis, but they are not the only fish to practice this method of reproduction. Some of the Callichthyid catfish – *Hoplosternum* and *Callichthys*, for instance – also construct bubble nests. These fish often live in oxygen-poor waters and the bubble nest allows the eggs to be kept near the surface of the water where there is more oxygen available to them. To construct the nest, the fish take in air at the water surface and blow bubbles in among the plants, sometimes shredding plants and incorporating bits of leaf into the nest. Set up the aquarium with plants, including some floating plants, and fill it about half full, because it is important to maintain high humidity above the water; otherwise, when the young fish come to the surface to take their first gulps of air, they will be chilled by the cold air and perish. With the Callichthyids, plants can be replaced by just about any floating object that will anchor the nest – bucket lids, acoustic tiles, and floating bark are most popular.

· · · · · EGG-SCATTERERS · · · · ·

These are usually shoal-spawning fish, such as barbs and characins, which produce large numbers of eggs, scattering them over fine-leaved plants or the substrate and then leaving them to fend for themselves. Some species lay adhesive eggs, which stick to plants; others lay non-adhesive eggs which fall to the bottom. In the aquarium, plant clumps of fine-leaved plants such as Java Moss for those with adhesive eggs. For the others, a layer of marbles on the bottom will allow the eggs to pass through but keep the parents away from them; alternatively, a piece of plastic mesh, cut the width of the tank but slightly longer can be placed in the aquarium before the shoal is put in for spawning. A clump of Java moss above this will afford the fish some privacy. The eggs will fall through the mesh and be safe from the adults.

Some egg scatterers are not shoal spawners, and these lay very few eggs at a time. Some of the killifish and the rainbowfish, for instance, can be bred quite easily using spawning mops. Construct the mops from yarn attached to a cork or a piece of styrofoam so that they float. The fish will lay the eggs among the strands of yarn. The mops can be removed from the spawning tanks and the young raised in separate tanks.

· · · · · SUBSTRATE SPAWNERS · · · · ·

These fish lay their eggs on a flat surface, such as a rock, a piece of wood or a leaf. Many also provide parental care, and clown fish, cichlids and some catfish are notable examples. The fish clean the surface before placing the eggs on it, and then tend them, insuring a good flow of oxygenated water over them and removing any damaged or infertile eggs. The fry are also guarded. These fish should be provided with a choice of suitable spawning sites, such as broad-leaved plants and flat stones. However, more often than not, the fish will clean the aquarium glass and use that. Although it is possible to remove the eggs and hatch them separately, in most cases the parents do a far better job. For fish which deposit their eggs on a flat surface but do not guard the eggs – for example, *Corydoras* – the parents can be removed and the eggs left to hatch. You must make sure that there is a flow of well-oxygenated water over the eggs.

· · · · · MOUTH-BROODERS · · · · ·

Either the male or the female, depending on the species, carries the eggs in the safety of their mouth in a brood pouch. While they are incubating the eggs, the adult does not feed. The young also seek refuge in the parent's mouth for quite some time after hatching. Some cichlids and some catfishes, the Asian Arowana (*Scleropages*), and Chocolate Gouramis are noted for this method of reproduction.

· · · · · NEST-BUILDERS · · · · ·

Fishes that carry out this form of reproduction actually modify their surroundings in order to breed. They may hollow out river banks and spawn in holes in the bank, as does *Pteryoplichthys*, or they may construct a depression in the substrate, banking larger stones around the edge, as does *Amia calva*, the Bowfin, or they may intertwine vegetation, as does the stickleback (*Gasterosteus*). The young ones are guarded.

RAISING THE FRY

Getting your fish to breed is only the first hurdle to overcome. The challenge often begins with raising the fry. It is impossible for the average person to cope with the 1,000-plus fry from a shoal spawning of *Danios*, so do not be disappointed if you cannot raise every last one. Do the best you can.

Before setting the fish up to spawn, make sure that you have everything you need – brine shrimp eggs and enough salt to provide the water to hatch them in, fine powdered foods and so forth. Setting up brine shrimp the same day that the fry need it is too late; you have to try and time things so that the shrimp is ready when the fry require it. You also need to have a battery of bottles to hatch sufficient quantities of shrimp in, old plastic soft-drink bottles are ideal; you will need four. Other requirements are four airstones, several yards of air line and an air pump. Set up the bottles as shown. You will need to feed the fry at night and in the morning, so you will be using two bottles a day and, as you use up one, you should restart it, ready for feeding in 48 hours time.

As the fry grow, you must increase the size of the food. Fine *Daphnia* is a welcome addition to the diet, and young fish will also start to take crumbled flake foods. As they grow, they will need to be split up into larger accommodation, so be prepared to set up more tanks!

ABOVE *Cichlids are noted for their parental care. This orange chromide,* Etroplus maculatus, *guards its brood against all comers.*

DIRECTORY
of
freshwater fish

CYPRINIDS

The cyprinids are a large group of freshwater fish which are distributed throughout North and Central America, Africa, Asia and Europe. Because of the value of some members as food fish, they have been widely introduced into other parts of the world, usually to the detriment of the endemic fauna.

Cyprinids do not have teeth on their jaws, but have a formidable set of pharygeal teeth which are set on the pharygeal bones just behind the gills and are used for grinding and crushing their food. The teeth are characteristic to each species. Cyprinids (and also the catfish and characins) possess the Weberian Apparatus, a linkeage of 3–4 pairs of bones connecting the swim bladder with the inner ear, which gives them very sensitive hearing, a facility which helps them avoid predators, or keep in touch with other members of a school. Their body shape is streamlined, covered with scales, with a single dorsal fin and no adipose fin. Some species, but by no means all, have a single spine on the leading edge of the dorsal, pectoral and anal fins. Many species also have barbels around the mouth.

The best-known members encountered in the aquatic hobby are Barbs, Rasboras, Danios and Carp.

BALANTIOCHEILUS MELANOPTERUS
(BLEEKER, 1851)

FAMILY: Cyprinidae

COMMON NAME: Silver Shark, Bala Shark

DISTRIBUTION: Southeast Asia

SIZE: 14in

COMPATIBILITY: Peaceful

6·5
▼
7·0 pH

pH: 6.5–7.0

dH: 5–10°

72°F
▼
80°F

TEMPERATURE: 72–80°F

BREEDING STRATEGY: Egg-layer

FOOD: Omnivore

This active fish requires a large aquarium with plenty of swimming space, so keep all planting to the sides and rear of the tank. If you use rocks and wood, avoid any sharp edges because these somewhat nervous fish may damage themselves if they knock against them when frightened. *B. melanopterus* is fond of jumping so make sure that the aquarium is well covered. The addition of a few floating plants may help to deter them from leaping out of the water. Despite their size, Silver Sharks are peaceful fish and can be kept with smaller species.

Most foods are taken, ranging from flake to frozen and freeze-dried. They also like some vegetable matter in their diet and will graze on the algae growing on plants or the aquarium glass. As an addition to their diet, live foods such as bloodworms and mosquito larvae are eagerly accepted.

These fish have not been bred in the aquarium, and little is known of their breeding habits. Females are believed to be deeper bodied than males during the breeding season.

BARBUS CALLIPTERUS
BOULENGER, 1907

FAMILY: Cyprinidae

COMMON NAME: Clipper Barb

DISTRIBUTION: West Africa from Cameroon to Niger

SIZE: 3½in

COMPATIBILITY: Peaceful

6·5 ▼ 7·5 pH

pH: 6.5–7.5

dH: to 25°

TEMPERATURE: 68–77°F

68°F ▼ 77°F

BREEDING STRATEGY: Egg-layer

FOOD: Omnivore

Clipper Barbs are quite hardy fish and will survive in most water conditions as long as extremes are avoided. It is a shoaling fish and is always active, cruising around the aquarium. In order to maintain the iridescent sheen on the body, small live foods must be included in the diet. Green foods also form part of the diet, and these barbs will nibble at the plants in the aquarium, although if you offer lettuce or peas, the amount of damage to the plants will be negligible.

When the fish are ready to spawn, females are generally fatter than males. It is only at this time that the sexes may be easily distinguished. Little is known of their breeding habits, although they appear to spawn in typical barb fashion by scattering their eggs over plants.

BARBUS FILAMENTOSUS
(VALENCIENNES, 1842)

FAMILY: Cyprinidae

COMMON NAME: Filament Barb

DISTRIBUTION: India, Sri Lanka

SIZE: 6in

COMPATIBILITY: Peaceful

pH: 6.0

6·0 pH

dH: to 15°

TEMPERATURE: 68–77°F

68°F ▼ 77°F

BREEDING STRATEGY: Egg-layer

FOOD: Omnivore

The juvenile coloration of this fish differs dramatically from that of the adult. Youngsters are very attractively colored, with two dark vertical bands on the body and red blotches in the dorsal, ventral and caudal fins. Adult males have an iridescent sheen to the body, which is tinged with green above and pink below. There is a dark spot almost on the posterior part of the flank. The dorsal fin has elongated rays (hence the specific name *filamentosus*). Males develop white tubercules on the upper lip and gills when they are in breeding condition. Females are quite drab by comparison and lack the fin ray extensions.

These are active fish and require a large aquarium with plenty of open water. They are greedy feeders and will take anything from algae and lettuce to live foods and chopped meat.

For breeding, provide a reasonably sized tank with a gravel substrate and a few clumps of fine-leaved plants. The water should be soft – say 8–10°dH – and slightly acidic – 6.0pH – with a temperature in the upper end of their range – 75–77°F. The fish spawn among the plants, but the parents are not averse to eating their eggs, so remove them after spawning. The eggs hatch within 36–48 hours. First fry foods are brine shrimp and powdered flake.

BARBUS SCHWANENFELDI
BLEEKER, 1853

FAMILY: Cyprinidae

COMMON NAME: Tinfoil Barb, Tinsel Barb

DISTRIBUTION: Widespread throughout Southeast Asia

SIZE: 14in

COMPATIBILITY: Peaceful

pH: 6.0–7.5

6·0
▼
7·5 pH

dH: to 18°

TEMPERATURE: 70–77°F

70 F
▼
77 F

BREEDING STRATEGY: Egg-layer

FOOD: Omnivore

Tinfoil Barbs are really only suitable for large aquaria. Inexperienced aquarists often buy small specimens because they do not realize the full growth potential of the fish. They are active school fish which require a large aquarium with an efficient filtration system. So that they may be seen at their best, the aquarium should be sparsely planted with the center left free for the school to display. Tinfoil Barbs should be introduced to a mature system because they do not seem happy with relatively new installations. If they are frightened, they will jump, but a few floating plants will help deter this and a heavy glass cover, known as "cour glasses" in the hobby, should be placed on the aquarium. The substrate should be sand or fine gravel because the fish grub in it searching for food.

Although they are peaceful, they will eat small fish, so you must make sure that any companions are of a suitable size. Their diet also consists of vegetable matter, live foods (insect larvae, for example), and flakes or pellets. Given reasonable conditions, growth can be rapid.

Sexual differences are not known, and, as yet, this fish has not been bred in the aquarium.

BARBUS TETRAZONA
(BLEEKER, 1855)

FAMILY: Cyprinidae

COMMON NAME: Tiger Barb, Sumatra Barb

DISTRIBUTION: Indonesia, Sumatra, Borneo

SIZE: 3in

COMPATIBILITY: May fin nip

pH: 6.5

6·5 pH

dH: to 12°

TEMPERATURE: 70–77°F

70°F
▼
77°F

BREEDING STRATEGY: Egg-layer

FOOD: Omnivore

Of all aquarium fish, Tiger Barbs probably have the worst reputation for fin nipping. It is possible to avoid trouble by keeping them in a school of 12 or more so that they are so busy picking on each other and establishing a pecking order within the school that they have no time for other fish. Alternatively, they can be kept in a species tank, where they make a wonderful sight.

Some color varieties have been bred: the Green Tiger Barb has an almost black body with an iridescent green sheen, and an albino strain has been established.

They require a reasonable amount of vegetable matter in their diet, and this can be provided by planting Java Moss in the aquarium and supplementing this with lettuce and peas. They are otherwise quite happy with flaked foods and the occasional treat of live foods.

Males are generally more colorful than females, and they are also slimmer. It is possible to breed them in the aquarium, but it may be difficult. The pairs should be in good condition, and the breeding aquarium should be furnished with a gravel substrate and some fine-leaved plants. The pH and dH of the water should be as above, but raise the temperature to 75–79°F.

Spawn is deposited over plants and hatches within 30 hours. When you select parents for breeding, try to make sure that only the best colored and best marked fish are used.

BARBUS TITTEYA
(DERANIYAGALA, 1929)

6·0 ▼ 7·5 pH

72°F ▼ 79°F

FAMILY: Cyprinidae

COMMON NAME: Cherry Barb

DISTRIBUTION: Sri Lanka

SIZE: 2in

COMPATIBILITY: Peaceful

pH: 6.0–7.5

dH: to 18°

TEMPERATURE: 72–79°F

BREEDING STRATEGY: Egg-layer

FOOD: Omnivore

Cherry Barbs are often shy and retiring, especially if their tank mates are boisterous. Provide a well-planted aquarium with thickets of fine-leaved plants for the fish to shelter in, but leave some open areas for swimming.

The smaller live foods and vegetable matter constitute the greater part of their diet, but they will also accept flake and small frozen foods.

Males are easily distinguished from females by their cherry red coloration, which intensifies during the breeding season. Females are brownish in color, darker on the dorsal surface with a narrow, dark brown line running along the flank from the tip of the snout, through the eye to the base of the caudal fin. When they are in breeding condition, there is an almost golden line of similar width just above the brown one. *B. titteya* can be bred in a small aquarium, using clumps of Java Moss. The water should be slightly acidic (at the lower end of the range), with a hardness of about 10° and a temperature in the range indicated above. Only a few eggs are deposited at a time, and these are attached to the plant by tiny threads. They hatch after about 24 hours, and the fry may be fed on infusoria, brine shrimp nauplii, or other suitable small foods.

♂

♀

BRACHYDANIO RERIO
(HAMILTON, 1822)

6·5 ▼ 7·0 pH

64°F ▼ 73°F

FAMILY: Cyprinidae

COMMON NAME: Zebra Danio, Zebra Fish

DISTRIBUTION: Eastern India

SIZE: 2½in

COMPATIBILITY: Peaceful

pH: 6.5–7.0

dH: 6–12°

TEMPERATURE: 64–73°F

BREEDING STRATEGY: Egg-layer

FOOD: Omnivore

Zebra Danios are widely available in the standard form and in the more recently developed albino and long-finned varieties. They should be kept as a school of about 10, in a planted aquarium that has plenty of open water, and because they are active fish, they appreciate a reasonable flow of water.

Zebra Danios are omnivorous and will eat anything from flake to algae. Vary the diet with live foods, lettuce and frozen foods to maintain them in good health.

Although they are school fish, breeding pairs tend to separate from the rest and shed their eggs over fine-leaved plants. Males are slimmer and more colorful than the females. Spawning takes place in the early morning and seems to be induced by early morning sunlight falling on the aquarium. Some 400 to 500 eggs are produced, and these hatch in about 48 hours. First foods are infusoria, brine shrimp nauplii, and powdered flake.

CROSSOCHEILUS SIAMENSIS
(SMITH, 1931)

FAMILY: Cyprinidae

COMMON NAME: Siamese Flying Fox

DISTRIBUTION: Southeast Asia, Thailand, Malay Peninsula

SIZE: 5½in

COMPATIBILITY: Peaceful

6·5 pH

pH: 6.5

dH: 5–10°

TEMPERATURE: 73–79°F

73°F ▼ 79°F

BREEDING STRATEGY: Egg-layer

FOOD: Herbivore

C. siamensis is both attractive and useful in the community aquarium, for they are active algae eaters. They require a planted aquarium, with mature, soft, slightly acidic, and well-oxygenated water. Given a reasonable flow of water, these fish will cavort about. To guarantee a good level of oxygen, use a spray bar on the return from a power filter. During hot weather, oxygen levels may decrease rapidly, and supplementary filtration may be required if the fish appear to be listless – resting on plants and breathing rapidly, for example.

Although they are herbivorous, these fish do not actually eat the plants; instead, they graze over the leaves, removing the soft algae. The only plant likely to be eaten is Java Moss, but this grows so quickly that even a small school of *C. siamensis* cannot keep up with it. The fish will also take flake foods and some of the smaller live foods, and they also like planarian worms.

The sexing and breeding of these creatures still remains a mystery.

DANIO AEQUIPINNATUS
(McCLELLAND, 1839)

FAMILY: Cyprinidae

COMMON NAME: Giant Danio

DISTRIBUTION: India and Sri Lanka

SIZE: 4in

COMPATIBILITY: Peaceful

5·5 ▼ 6·5 pH

pH: 5.5–6.5

dH: 2–12°

TEMPERATURE: 70–75°F

70°F ▼ 75°F

BREEDING STRATEGY: Egg-layer

FOOD: Omnivore

A delightful species for larger community aquaria, these fish require a planted aquarium with plenty of open water. Good water movement is beneficial, because they like to swim against a gentle current.

These omnivores will consume most proprietary fish foods, but the addition of live foods to their diet will enhance their colors. Males are much slimmer than the females, and the blue line in their body runs straight into the caudal fin. In females the blue stripe bends upward at the base of the caudal, and females are less brilliantly colored than males and have much thicker bodies.

To induce them to spawn, keep them in a large aquarium with fresh water and anchor some bunches of fine-leaved plants in the substrate. Put the females into the tank first and introduce the males a day or so later. The fish usually spawn in early morning when the first rays of sunlight fall on the tank. After spawning, remove the parents, as they will often eat the eggs. Hatching occurs after 24–36 hours. First foods are newly hatched brine shrimp. If they are well fed the fry grow rapidly.

EPALZEORHYNCHUS KALLOPTERUS
BLEEKER, 1850

FAMILY: Cyprinidae

COMMON NAME: Flying Fox

DISTRIBUTION: Sumatra, Borneo, Thailand, Indonesia

SIZE: 6in

COMPATIBILITY: Peaceful

pH: 6.5–7.0

6·5 ▼ 7·0 pH

dH: 8–10°

TEMPERATURE: 72–79°F

72°F ▼ 79°F

BREEDING STRATEGY: Egg-layer

FOOD: Omnivore

These active fish come from fast-flowing streams, and they therefore require a good movement of well-oxygenated water. They prefer to be kept in groups rather than as solitary specimens and will often be seen darting around and chasing each other. They can be territorial, so provide wood, rocks and broad-leaved plants, on which they will rest, holding the front of their bodies just off the surface by using their pectoral fins. Each fish will stake out a territory and, should another encroach on it, will chase it off, but rarely is any damage done to either party.

Flying Foxes browse on soft algae and will also accept lettuce, peas, flake and small live foods.

Nothing is known of sexing these creatures, and they have not been bred in the aquarium.

RASBORA HETEROMORPHA
DUNCKER, 1904

FAMILY: Cyprinidae

COMMON NAME: Harlequin Fish, Red Rasbora

DISTRIBUTION: Southeast Asia

SIZE: 1¾in

COMPATIBILITY: Peaceful

pH: 5.5–6.5

5·5 ▼ 6·5 pH

dH: 2–12°

TEMPERATURE: 72–77°F

72°F ▼ 77°F

BREEDING STRATEGY: Egg-layer

FOOD: Insectivore

A lively, school fish for the community aquarium, *R. heteromorpha* should be kept in a well-planted aquarium and in a group of eight or more specimens. Although they will accept flake, frozen and freeze-dried foods, they should be given live foods to maintain the almost metallic sheen on their bodies.

The sexes are easy to distinguish: not only is the male slimmer, the leading edge of the markings on the male is slightly rounded at the base, while on the female it is straight.

Breeding is difficult but possible if you are prepared to provide the exacting conditions they require. Prepare a shallow spawning aquarium using a fine substrate, some broad-leaved plants, such as *Cryptocoryne* species, and soft – 2°dH – acid – pH 5.3–5.6 – water. Maintain a temperature of 79–80°F and filter over peat. The breeding aquarium should be set up at least a month before you intend to try to spawn the fish. Choose a young female (many attempts at breeding have failed through using an older female) and an older male. The pair spawn on the underside of leaves when swimming inverted. After spawning, remove the parents and darken the tank. The eggs hatch in 24 hours, and first foods for the fry are infusoria.

CHARACINS

Characins are found throughout South and Central America, and their range extends as far north as Texas in the US. They are also widely distributed in Africa. They are popular aquarium fish, and some of the best-known are small and very colorful, the Neon Tetra (Paracheirodon innesi) and the Cardinal Tetra (Cheirodon axelrodi), for example. Many of the larger members form an important role in the food fish and sport fish industries of their native lands.

This large group of freshwater fish, which look externally very similar to the cyprinids, have, in common with them and the catfish, the Weberian Apparatus. Their body form varies, but all have cycloid scales. They can be distinguished from cyprinids in that they do not have barbels; their teeth, often very well developed, are firmly attached to their jaws and the mouth is not protractile. Most, but not all, characins have an adipose fin which is situated well back on the body close to the caudal peduncle.

In the main, characins are carnivores, varying from insectivores to the flesh-eating Piranhas. There are, however, a few herbivores such as the giant Pacu.

ANOSTOMUS ANOSTOMUS
(LINNAEUS, 1758)

FAMILY: Anostomidae

COMMON NAME: Striped Anostomus

DISTRIBUTION: Amazon, Orinoco, Venezuela, Guyana, Colombia

SIZE: 7in

COMPATIBILITY: Usually peaceful

6·5 ▼ 7·0 pH

pH: 6.5–7.0

dH: 8–10°

72°F ▼ 79°F

TEMPERATURE: 72–79°F

BREEDING STRATEGY: Egg-layer

FOOD: Omnivore

A. anostomus have a reputation for picking on other fish. However, this is probably because they tend to be kept in small groups of three or four individual fish, while if a single specimen were to be kept in a community aquarium, it would tolerate its tank mates. Alternatively, these fish should be kept in larger groups of eight or more. They require a well-planted aquarium with plenty of rocks to simulate their natural habitat – they live in almost vertical fissures in the rocks, in fast-flowing water where the water is shallow and the algal growth lush. A good water current is also beneficial.

In the aquarium lettuce and spinach can be offered as substitutes for algae so that they do not destroy all your plants. They will still pick at any algae that does grow in the aquarium. Alternative and supplementary foods are vegetable flakes, live foods such as *Daphnia* and mosquito larvae, and some of the frozen foods.

They are believed to have been bred, but no details have been found of sexual differences or of spawning itself.

ARNOLDICHTHYS SPILOPTERUS
(BOULENGER, 1909)

FAMILY: Alestidae

COMMON NAME: Red-eyed Characin

DISTRIBUTION: West Africa (Lagos to the Niger delta)

SIZE: 3¼in

COMPATIBILITY: Community

6·0
▼
7·5 pH

pH: 6.0–7.5

dH: to 20°

73°F
▼
82°F

TEMPERATURE: 73–82°F

BREEDING STRATEGY: Egg-layer

FOOD: Insectivore

This peaceful school fish is ideal for the larger community aquarium. Furnish the tank with groups of plants, but make sure that there are open areas in which these active fish can swim. They should be kept in groups of eight or more, and make sure that you have males and females so that you see them at their best. They are easily sexable: males have a convex anal fin with red, yellow and black stripes, while females have nearly straight anal fins.

Red-eyed characins will accept most proprietary flake and frozen foods, but they do appreciate the inclusion of live food in their diet. To maintain them in good condition, it is important that the water is changed regularly. If slightly cooler water is used to replace the water that is removed, there is every chance that well-conditioned, adult fish will spawn. Up to 1,000 eggs may be laid by a single pair. The eggs hatch in about 30 hours, with the fry free swimming after a week. Experience has shown that they prefer softer water for breeding – 6–8°dH was the favored range – and a temperature drop from 75°F to about 66°F was a stimulus about 24 hours prior to spawning. Spawning took place over fine-leaved plants in sunlight.

BOULENGERELLA MACULATA
(VALENCIENNES, 1849)

FAMILY: Ctenoliciidae

COMMON NAME: Pike Characin

DISTRIBUTION: Amazon tributaries

SIZE: 14in

COMPATIBILITY: Predator

6·0
▼
7·5 pH

pH: 6.0–7.5

dH: to 18°

TEMPERATURE: 73–79°F

73°F
▼
79°F

BREEDING STRATEGY: Egg-layer

FOOD: Piscivore

A surface-dwelling characin, this fish is for the specialist. It requires a large tank with plenty of open water for swimming but also some secluded areas, which can be provided by broad-leaved plants, by bog wood and vine roots or by a combination of both. Highly oxygenated water is also necessary, and the use of external power filters coupled with trickle filters can provide this.

Young fish are more easily acclimatized than adults, which are timid and easy frightened. Any sudden movement near the aquarium will scare them, and they are prone to damage their bodies and snouts. They may also leap from the water if any attempt to catch them by bringing the net up from below is made.

Juveniles will eventually take flake foods, but they prefer insect larvae and small fish. As the Pike Characin grows, it will require progressively larger foods. Be prepared to feed live fish as a last resort.

CARNEGIELLA STRIGATA
(GUENTHER, 1864)

FAMILY: Gasteropelecidae

COMMON NAME: Marbled Hatchetfish

DISTRIBUTION: Peru

SIZE: 1½in

COMPATIBILITY: Peaceful

pH: 5.5–7.0

dH: to 20°

5·5
▼
7·0 pH

TEMPERATURE: 73–82°F

73°F
▼
82°F

BREEDING STRATEGY: Egg-layer

FOOD: Insectivore

Hatchetfish are popular aquarium fish, but they can be very difficult to keep. They need to be kept as a school of six or more, and although they will accept flake food, they do not thrive on it and must have copious amounts of live foods, such as bloodworm and mosquito larvae, and/or similar frozen foods in their diet. They

inhabit the upper levels of the aquarium and will often be seen in the outflow from the filter return pipes. Make sure that you have a tight-fitting cover glass because they jump!

For breeding, the water should be soft and acidic. Females have a greater girth than males, and when they are close to spawning, it may be possible to see the eggs. The fish dart about the aquarium and eventually place the eggs on the roots of floating plants. Some eggs may fall to the bottom. Remove the parents, which may eat the eggs. Hatching occurs after some 30 hours, and the fry are free-swimming after five days. First foods include infusoria, *Paramecium* and, later, brine shrimp nauplii.

DISTICHODUS SEXFASCIATUS
BOULENGER, 1897

FAMILY: Citharinidae

DISTRIBUTION: Zaire basin; Angola

SIZE: 10in

COMPATIBILITY: Peaceful with fish of similar size

pH: 6.0–7.5

dH: 10–20°

6·0
▼
7·5 pH

TEMPERATURE: 72–79°F

BREEDING STRATEGY: Egg-layer

72°F
▼
79°F

FOOD: Vegetarian

D. sexfasciatus needs to be kept in an aquarium at least 5ft long. They are most attractive in their juvenile form, when the red fins and dark bars on the body are extremely eyecatching. However, this fades as the fish matures, and they become grayish-

yellow. A species tank is ideal for these creatures, and as it is impossible to tell the sexes apart, it may prove to be the only way of successfully spawning them in captivity.

Although vegetarian, they are omnivorous in captivity, eating anything from flake to frozen foods. However, it is wise to make sure that vegetable matter predominates in their diet. Keep them in a planted aquarium, and as long as you provide enough green foods in the form of peas, lettuce and so on, they will leave the plants alone. Java Fern, various species of Amazon Swordplants, some of the *Cryptocoryne* species, and any other hard-leaved plants stand a good chance of survival, especially if they are well established before the fish are introduced to the aquarium. Avoid soft-leaved plants – *Cabomba*, *Ludwigia arcuata*, and *Micracanthemum micracanthamoides*, for example – as these will be eaten.

LEPIDARCHUS ADONIS
ROBERTS, 1966

FAMILY: Alestidae

COMMON NAME: Jellybean Tetra

DISTRIBUTION: West Africa

SIZE: ¾in

COMPATIBILITY: Peaceful but should be kept only with other small peaceful fish

5·8 ▼ 6·5 pH

pH: 5.8–6.5

dH: 4–6°

72°F ▼ 79°F

TEMPERATURE: 72–79°F

BREEDING STRATEGY: Egg-layer

FOOD: Small invertebrates

L. adonis is a beautiful small fish for the specialist, and if it is to survive in captivity, it must be kept in extremely soft, acidic water of the highest quality. In addition, the aquarium should be heavily planted with fine-leaved plants and reasonably well lit.

Males are easily identified: their transparent bodies have several purple-brown spots on the rear half, while females have virtually transparent, almost glassy bodies. These fish are not prolific, but if they are kept in very soft water at about 77°F, they will breed. About 20–30 eggs are laid on the plants. These hatch in about 36 hours, but the fry are not free-swimming for five or six days. Despite their small size, they will take newly hatched brine shrimp nauplii.

Feeding is simple, for the adults will take any suitable small foods, although they require live foods, such as fine *Daphnia* and *Cyclops*, to bring them into breeding condition.

MOENKHAUSIA PITTERI
EIGENMANN, 1920

FAMILY: Characidae

COMMON NAME: Diamond Tetra

DISTRIBUTION: Venezuela

SIZE: 2½in

COMPATIBILITY: Peaceful, community

pH: 5.5–7.0

5·5 ▼ 7·0 pH

dH: 4–10°

TEMPERATURE: 75–82°F

75°F ▼ 82°F

BREEDING STRATEGY: Egg-layer

FOOD: Insectivore

When they are offered for sale, young Diamond Tetras look just like any other nondescript fish. It is only with age that the finnage develops and they take on their colorful hues. The best way of acquiring good-quality adult fish is to buy a school of 15–20 youngsters and to grow them on. Given a copious, high quality diet, including live foods, they will grow rapidly. Adult fish can be sexed: males have longer, more pointed dorsal fins and more intense coloration. In order to condition them for breeding, live mosquito larvae and bloodworms should be included in the diet.

They like a planted tank with some darker areas for seclusion. A gentle current is also appreciated, and this can be provided either by powerheads or by external filters.

Soft, acidic water is required for breeding. Before spawning there is much displaying by the males in the school. This is especially spectacular if it is seen in sunlight, when it is very easy to see how they get their common name, Diamond Tetra. The eggs are deposited on fine-leaved plants – Java Moss is ideal for this purpose – and they hatch a couple of days later. After the yolk sac is absorbed, the fry can be fed on newly hatched brine shrimp nauplii. The parents will often eat their own eggs, so, if they are breeding in a community tank and using Java moss, the plant and eggs can be removed for hatching and raising separately, although you must be sure to use water from the parents' tank in the new tank.

NANNOSTOMUS EQUES
(STEINDACHNER, 1876)

FAMILY: Lebiasinidae

COMMON NAME: Three-striped Pencilfish

DISTRIBUTION: Rio Negro, northern Brazil

SIZE: 2in

COMPATIBILITY: Peaceful

pH: 5.5–6.5

dH: 4–10°

TEMPERATURE: 73–79°F

BREEDING STRATEGY: Egg-layer

FOOD: Insectivore

5·5
▼
6·5 pH

73°F
▼
79°F

This delightful school fish is easy to keep in a community tank of similar-sized fishes. If you keep them in a group of 10 or so, they will always be seen because they appear to get confidence from each other. If one or two specimens are kept, they retreat to the darker areas of the tank and remain there. They swim near the surface, their bodies at an angle and their heads pointing up.

Pencilfish have nocturnal coloration, which is species specific, and it takes the form of transverse bands. If you happen to switch on the tank lights after a period of darkness, do not be alarmed if your fish appear to have changed their color pattern – there is nothing wrong with them.

Males may be distinguished by their more intense coloration and slimmer bodies. They may be bred in captivity. Put pairs in a separate breeding tank containing both broad- and fine-leaved plants. The male drives the female quite hard before a few eggs are released. Feed the fry on rotifers or the smallest brine shrimp nauplii.

PHAGO MACULATUS
AHL, 1922

FAMILY: Citharinidae

COMMON NAME: African Pike Characin

DISTRIBUTION: Niger delta, West Africa

SIZE: 5½in

COMPATIBILITY: Predator

pH: 6.5–7.5

dH: to 20°

TEMPERATURE: 72–80°F

BREEDING STRATEGY: Egg-layer

FOOD: Carnivore

6·5
▼
7·5 pH

72°F
▼
80°F

This elongated characin is seldom imported and is a fish for the specialist. It is a voracious predator, and it should be kept either alone or with larger, quiet fish. Like most predators, it lurks among roots and vegetation to ambush its prey. Create a similar environment in the aquarium, using plants and vine roots. If the fish feels secure it will feed, but if the tank contains other boisterous fish or if there is insufficient cover, it will refuse to feed.

Small specimens may be offered small live foods, including insect larvae, but as it matures *P. maculatus* will consume whole live fish. Reports from the wild have indicated that it is not unknown for it to attack and feed on the caudal fins of other large fish.

Nothing is known of this species' breeding habits or of distinguishing the sexes.

PHENACOGRAMMUS INTERRUPTUS
(BOULENGER, 1899)

FAMILY: Alestiidae

COMMON NAME: Congo Tetra, Congo Salmon

DISTRIBUTION: Zaire

SIZE: male 3–3½in; female 2½in

COMPATIBILITY: Peaceful, community

pH: 6.0–6.2

6·0 ▼ 6·2 pH

dH: 4–15°

TEMPERATURE: 75–80°F

75°F ▼ 80°F

BREEDING STRATEGY: Egg-layer

FOOD: Insectivore

This beautiful African characin should be kept in an aquarium 4ft or more long. Good filtration is essential because these fish will not tolerate a build-up of nitrates in the aquarium. Buy a school of eight or so young specimens. They are quite dull and uninteresting at this stage, but they have the advantage of being much cheaper to buy than adult fish. Initially, the juveniles will not have the well-developed finnage or color of the adults, but with correct feeding, good conditions and time, they will grow into prime specimens. As with the majority of fish, the males develop the better colors and longer finnage.

These are active fish and require an aquarium that has plenty of swimming space and that is well planted – they sometimes like to nibble at softer leaved plants, but do no real damage. If conditions are right – soft, slightly acid water and some fine-leaved plants such as Java Moss – the fish will spawn in a community aquarium. If this happens, do not expect to raise any fry, as the other fish will eagerly devour the eggs. They can, however, be successfully bred in a separate aquarium. A pair will produce up to 300 eggs, which hatch in about six days. First foods are infusoria, followed by newly hatched brine shrimp. To keep the fish in peak condition, mosquito larvae are essential and will be avidly consumed. All smaller live foods are acceptable, as are flake and frozen foods.

SEMAPROCHILODUS TAENIURUS
(VALENCIENNES, 1817)

FAMILY: Curimatidae

DISTRIBUTION: Western Colombia and Brazil

SIZE: 12in

COMPATIBILITY: Peaceful

pH: 5.5–7.5

dH: to 20°

5·5 ▼ 7·5 pH

TEMPERATURE: 72–79°F

BREEDING STRATEGY: Egg-layer

72°F ▼ 79°F

FOOD: Predominantly vegetarian

This large, extremely active species, likes the company of its own kind, so keep two or three together. They make excellent companions for some of the larger, non-aggressive catfish.

If they are to be kept with any degree of success, it is important to have a good, efficient filtration system. External power filters are ideal because they also provide a good flow of water in the aquarium, and *S. taeniurus* loves to swim against currents. They are also easily frightened, and a sturdy cover is advisable.

They can be difficult to acclimatize to life in captivity, the main problem apparently being the need to get the water quality right. Feeding is not normally an obstacle: they take flake, tablet and some frozen foods, such as bloodworms as well as green foods. Frozen peas seem to be a particular delicacy. Despite their love of vegetable matter, it is possible to keep them in a planted aquarium as long as you choose the plants with care – *Cryptocoryne* species, Amazon Swordplants and Java Fern are tough enough to stand up to them as, surprisingly, is Java Moss, which grows so fast that the constant grazing keeps it in check.

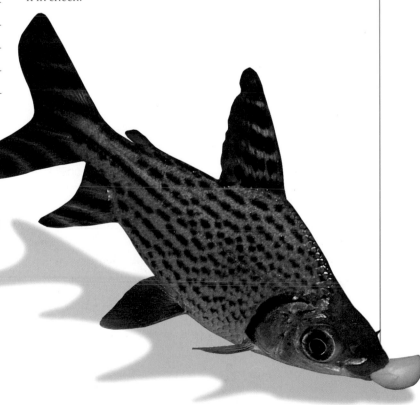

SERRASALMUS NATTERERI
KNER, 1859

FAMILY: Serrasalmidae

COMMON NAME: Red Piranha

DISTRIBUTION: Parana River basin, South America

SIZE: to 12in

COMPATIBILITY: Predator

5·5
▼
7·5 pH

pH: 5.5–7.5

dH: to 20°

72°F
▼
79°F

TEMPERATURE: 72–79°F

BREEDING STRATEGY: Egg-layer

FOOD: Carnivore

Piranhas are reputed to strip the flesh from bones and to eat anything at all, especially when they are hungry. They are best kept in a species tank, and you can keep a small school of them provided you keep up a steady supply of food. The aquarium must be large, more than 4ft long, and the filtration system must be very efficient to cope with high protein waste from these voracious carnivores. They appreciate a good flow of water, and this is easily provided if you use external filtration systems.

Feeding poses no problems – pieces of meat, fish, whole shrimps and so on are eagerly devoured. The only problem that may arise is in keeping up with the quantity of food that is required by 8–10 hungry fish. Take extra care when handling them. They have formidable teeth, and fingers are easy prey. They will not hesitate to attack if they feel threatened.

Piranhas have been bred in captivity, but only in very large aquaria. They spawn in the early morning, and the male and female then guard the nest for 24 hours. The male then chases the female away, but he continues to guard the 500–1,000 eggs. First foods are newly hatched brine shrimp. As the fry grow, they should be sorted by size before the larger ones become cannibalistic.

Many public aquaria display large schools of these creatures, and they are a great attraction.

EGG-LAYING TOOTHCARPS OR KILLIFISH

This group of fish is found in tropical and warmer temperate regions of the world with the exception of Australia. They are predominantly freshwater fish, although one or two species are found in brackish waters. Their name Toothcarps infers that they are relatives of the carps, but this is not the case as they lack the Weberian Apparatus and also have fine teeth on their jaws.

Toothcarps are sometimes referred to as Killifish or Top-minnows. Their heads are usually flattened, and they have a wide, terminal, protrusible mouth. They lack an adipose fin and have no lateral line organs. The dorsal fin is usually set about halfway along their back.

They are adaptable creatures able to tolerate a wide range of temperatures, water salinity and drought. Some are "annual" fish, in that when their seasonal pools dry up the adults perish, but their fertilized eggs lie dormant, buried in the soil where they remain until the rains return.

Male Killifish have the brightest colors, which makes them highly desirable as aquarium fish but, in order to see them at their best, make sure that there are some of the drabber females present for them to display to. The added bonus is the chance of breeding.

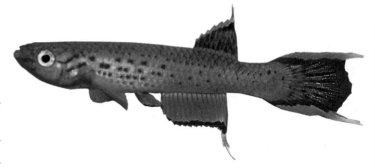

APHYOSEMION AUSTRALE
(RACHOW, 1921)

FAMILY: Cyprinodontidae

COMMON NAME: Cape Lopez Lyretail, Lyretail, Lyre-tailed Panchax

DISTRIBUTION: West Africa

SIZE: 2½in

COMPATIBILITY: Peaceful

pH: 5.5–6.5

dH: to 10°

TEMPERATURE: 70–75°F

BREEDING STRATEGY: Egg-layer

FOOD: Insectivore

5·5 ▼ 6·5 pH

70°F ▼ 75°F

A. australe is best kept in a species tank if you intend to breed them. They can be included in a community aquarium, but great care has to be taken over the choice of companions because the males' magnificent finnage is often bitten and nipped by other fish. These fish are usually sold as pairs, a brilliantly colored male with fin extensions and a much drabber female with more normal shaped finnage. It is often impossible to tell the female of one species from the female of another so, to avoid interbreeding, they should be kept in a species aquarium.

If you provide a soft loam substrate, fine-leaved plants, soft, acid water, low temperatures and plenty of live foods, the fish will thrive. During the warmest part of the year, they can be kept without any additional heating in the aquarium. Eggs are laid in the substrate or on the lower parts of plants. These should be removed each day, and they can be treated in the same way as those of other annual fish – that is, keep them in the dry peat for about three months, wet the peat and the fry should hatch. First foods are brine shrimp nauplii.

APHYOSEMION SJOESTEDTI
(LOENNBERG, 1895)

FAMILY: Cyprinodontidae

COMMON NAME: Red Aphyosemion, Golden Pheasant

DISTRIBUTION: West Africa

SIZE: 5in

COMPATIBILITY: Can be aggressive

pH: 6.0–6.5

dH: to 12°

TEMPERATURE: 73–79°F

BREEDING STRATEGY: Egg-layer

FOOD: Insectivore

6·0 ▼ 6·5 pH

73°F ▼ 79°F

As with all *Aphyosemion* sp., the males are more colorful than the females and, in this species at least, considerably larger. *A. sjoestedti* is suited to a well-planted, larger community aquarium with tank mates of a similar size and disposition to itself. Sometimes *A sjoestedti* can be aggressive and boisterous, especially if they are trying to breed in the community tank. It is fairly tolerant of water conditions and will accept all the normal commercially prepared foods, but to see them at their best provide a varied diet which includes live foods.

To breed, adults should be conditioned well on all forms of live foods prior to introducing them to the breeding aquarium. Being one of the larger killifish, this species requires a fairly large tank. Males can be quarrelsome, especially at this time. Use one male to two females to prevent a single female from being chased too hard. Provide plenty of plant cover and a thick covering of peat on the bottom. A water temperature in the region of 73°F, plus or minus one degree, a pH of 6.5, and a hardness of about 10° is considered suitable. When spawning, the fish press their eggs into the substrate. Once spawning is completed, the eggs and peat are removed, the excess moisture is squeezed from it and the peat/egg mixture stored in a plastic bag for four to six weeks. During this time, maintain a temperature of about 68°F, and make sure that the peat does not dry out completely. After this time, add soft water to induce hatching. The young may be fed on newly hatched brine shrimp. Growth is fairly rapid, especially if a regime of regular water changes is maintained.

APLOCHEILUS LINEATUS
(VALENCIENNES, 1846)

FAMILY: Cyprinondontidae

COMMON NAME: Striped Panchax

DISTRIBUTION: Southern India

SIZE: 3¼in

COMPATIBILITY: Can be aggressive

pH: 6.0–7.0

dH: to 11°

6·0 ▼ 7·0 pH

TEMPERATURE: 72–80°F

72°F ▼ 80°F

BREEDING STRATEGY: Egg-layer

FOOD: Insectivore/piscivore

This surface-dwelling killifish is an active predator, which will take any insects that fall on the water surface as well as aquatic insects and small fish. It is suitable only for aquaria with fish of its own size. They also jump, so make sure you cover the aquarium, and you should also provide some floating plants, because they love to lurk among the roots.

Both sexes are attractive, although the male is brighter and has more flowing fins. The female has six or eight narrow, black vertical bands on the rear of the body and lacks the intensity of gold speckling shown on the male.

They can be easily bred in a community aquarium using spawning mops. The fish will deposit their eggs on them; the mop can then be removed to another aquarium filled with water from the parents' tank and hatched there. The eggs hatch in about 12 days, and the fry can be fed on newly hatched brine shrimp, fine *Daphnia* and crushed flake.

JORDANELLA FLORIDAE
GOODE & BEAN, 1879

FAMILY: Cyprinodontidae

COMMON NAME: American Flagfish

DISTRIBUTION: Florida and southern USA to Yucatan, Mexico

SIZE: 2½in

COMPATIBILITY: Can be aggressive

6·5 ▼ 7·5 pH

pH: 6.5–7.5

dH: to 18°

68°F ▼ 70°F

TEMPERATURE: 68–70°F

BREEDING STRATEGY: Egg-layer

FOOD: Omnivore

This cool-water killifish is often overlooked in favor of its more colorful tropical relations. The olive to red-brown males are brightly colored and have iridescent green on their flanks and red spreading into the dorsal, anal and ventral fins. Females in contrast are larger and deeper in the body, more yellow in color and have a dark spot in the dorsal fin.

Males can be very aggressive toward each other and, in consequence, when they are offered for sale they make a sorry sight because they may have nipped fins and, due to harassing each other, tend not to show their best colors.

They need a well-planted aquarium with an open area for swimming and some clear areas of substrate. Use fine gravel or coarse sand on the bottom. Place the aquarium where sunlight will fall on it, and do not worry if you get algae growing on the sides because this forms an essential part of the fish's diet. They are true omnivores and will take live foods, detritus, algae, bits of chopped meat and lettuce.

Courtship can be violent. The male chivvies and nips at the female. The eggs are laid either on the lower parts of the plants close to the substrate or on the substrate itself. Sometimes the male guards the eggs and fry, driving the female away; sometimes both parents will care for the brood, so be guided by the behavior of your fish. Hatching occurs after about a week, and the fry are easy to raise on microworms, newly hatched brine shrimp, powdered foods and so on.

NOTHOBRANCHIUS RACHOVII
AHL, 1926

FAMILY: Cyprinodontidae

COMMON NAME: Rachow's Nothobranch

DISTRIBUTION: Mozambique to South Africa

SIZE: 2in

COMPATIBILITY: Usually peaceful, but can be belligerent to its own kind

pH: 6.5

dH: 4–6°

TEMPERATURE: 68–75°F

BREEDING STRATEGY: Egg-layer

FOOD: Insectivore

6·5 pH

68°F
▼
70°F

N. rachovii is short-lived, one of a group of annual killifish whose natural habitat dries out each year, and its mode of reproduction reflects this. Males are highly colored, whereas females are dull brown and much smaller. When breeding, males can become territorial and somewhat aggressive.

Nothobranchius are substrate spawners. In the wild the pair dive into the substrate and deposit their eggs, which remain there as the ponds dry out and the parents perish. When the rains return, not all the eggs hatch at once, perhaps a few with the first downpour, which may only be enough to wet the ground and create a puddle which then dries out again. The remainder will wait until the rains are well established and there is enough water to allow the fry to grow to maturity and breed. The fish are sexually mature in a matter of only 12 weeks.

To imitate these conditions in home aquaria, use a peat substrate. The fish will spawn in this and it can then be removed, squeezed out so that it is just moist, and stored in a plastic bag for three or four months. Do remember to label the bag with the species name and date of spawning. Add water, and the fry should hatch. If you only get a few at this first wetting, repeat the process and store for a little longer; then wet the peat again – you will have imitated nature with the first and second rains.

As the adults spawn virtually constantly, feeding is very important. Use only high-quality foods and whenever possible copious amounts of live food, such as *Daphnia* and mosquito larvae. Poor-quality adults will result in poor-quality fry, and after a few generations your stock may become stunted.

RIVULUS CYLINDRACEUS
POEY, 1861

FAMILY: Cyprinodontidae

COMMON NAME: Green Rivulus, Brown Rivulus, Cuban Rivulus

DISTRIBUTION: Cuba

SIZE: 2¼in

COMPATIBILITY: Fairly peaceful

pH: 7.0

dH: to 10°

TEMPERATURE: 72–75°F

BREEDING STRATEGY: Egg-layer

FOOD: Insectivore

7·0 pH

72°F
▼
75°F

A very active species which makes a welcome addition to a community tank of other peaceful species of similar size. The aquarium should be decorated with fine-leaved plants. Floating plants are advantageous as these fish will often jump. The fish also like to lurk in caves and hollows, or beneath plants and wood.

Most foods are acceptable from flakes to frozen. To see the fish in their best colors, however, provide copious amounts of live foods in the form of mosquito larvae, bloodworm, *Tubifex* and fruit flies.

To breed them in any quantity, first condition the prospective parents separately. If possible, use one male and two females. Set a small aquarium with a covering of gravel on the bottom and plenty of fine-leaved plants and/or spawning mops. Add water and maintain a temperature in the region of 75°F. Place the conditioned adults in the breeding aquarium and, usually in the early morning, the fish will spawn, placing the eggs on the fine-leaved plants or mops. The males drive fairly hard – hence the reason for using two females, to prevent one from becoming too harassed. The eggs hatch in about a fortnight, and the resultant fry have a characteristic dark line running from head to tail. On hatching they will take newly hatched brine shrimp almost immediately, and growth is rapid, especially if regular water changes are carried out.

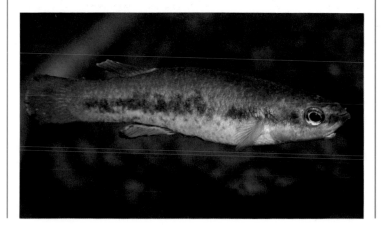

LIVE-BEARING TOOTHCARPS

Found from the southern states of the US through Central America and into South America, these tooth-carps differ from the Killifish in that they give birth to live young. The anal fin of the males is modified into a movable gonapodium. Either all the rays, or the first few rays, form a tube through which the sperm is transferred to the cloaca of the female. Fertilization takes place within the female's body, and one fertilization can produce several generations of young. The young develop within the female's ovarian cavity and when born are still in the egg, but the egg membrane ruptures almost immediately. This method of reproduction is known as ovoviparity.

The ease of breeding these fish and their rapid growth has led to them being line-bred to enhance one or other of their features. The Guppy, for example, has been bred to enhance the color and shape of the caudal fir of the males, and the creature we now see as being a "standard" Guppy is almost unrecognizable when compared with its wild counterpart. Swordtails, Platies and Mollies have also been treated in a similar manner.

ANABLEPS ANABLEPS
(LINNAEUS, 1756)

7·0 ▼ 8·5 pH

75°F ▼ 80°F

FAMILY:	Anablepidae
COMMON NAME:	Four-eyed Fish
DISTRIBUTION:	Central America, northern South America
SIZE:	12in
COMPATIBILITY:	Peaceful
pH:	7.0–8.5
dH:	to 30°
TEMPERATURE:	75–80°F
BREEDING STRATEGY:	Live-bearer
FOOD:	Carnivore

A surface-dwelling live-bearer, *A. anableps* is well suited to its environment. In the wild it inhabits fresh and brackish waters, but in an aquarium it does best in warm, brackish water. The water should be shallow, only 8–12in deep, but the aquarium should be large, with plenty of open water because these are lively school fish. They feed on insects and will even jump from the water to catch them. They require copious amounts of live foods, such as flies, as well as aquatic insect larvae – for example, mosquito larvae – although they will also take flakes.

Males have a modified anal fin, or gonopodium, which is fairly inflexible, and the male can move it to one side only, which means that a male with a right-handed gonopodium can mate only with a female whose sex organs open to the left, and vice versa. They breed best in warm (80–84°F), shallow water (4–6in), and the young are about 1in when born.

The most notable features of this fish are the eyes, which have an upper and a lower part; the upper portion is for vision above water and allows fish to detect food and, more importantly, predators such as birds, while the lower portion lets it see underwater.

POECILIA LATIPINNA
(LESUEUR, 1821)

FAMILY: Poeciliidae

COMMON NAME: Sailfin Molly

DISTRIBUTION: Southern USA, Mexico

SIZE: Males 4in; females 4¾in

COMPATIBILITY: Peaceful

pH: 7.5–8.5

7·5
▼
8·5 pH

dH: 25–35°

TEMPERATURE: 77–80°F

77°F
▼
80°F

BREEDING STRATEGY: Live-bearer

FOOD: Herbivore

Mollies are usually considered ideal fish for community aquaria, but, in fact, nothing could be further from the truth. They are very demanding of water conditions, requiring hard, alkaline waters with some salt needed. *P. latipinna* and its close relative *P. velifera* (the two can be distinguished by the number of dorsal fin rays: *P. latipinna* has 14, *P. velifera* has 18–19) are frequently used to mature marine systems. They also make ideal fish for brackish water aquaria.

Algae is an important part of their diet, although they will also take live, flake and frozen foods. If you have insufficient algae in the aquarium, offer lettuce and peas as a supplement.

They breed easily and will not normally eat their young. However, any attempt to confine the pregnant female in a breeding trap could result in her death. It is far better to provide cover for the fry in the parents' tank.

P. latipinna and *P. velifera* cross easily. Many color forms have been developed for the aquatic trade, and even lyre-tailed forms have been offered for sale.

BELONESOX BELIZANUS
KNER, 1860

FAMILY: Poeciliidae

COMMON NAME: Piketop Live-bearer, Piketop Minnow

DISTRIBUTION: Eastern Central America

SIZE: Male 4¾in; female 8in

COMPATIBILITY: Can be aggressive

7·5
▼
8·2 pH

pH: 7.5–8.2

dH: above 25°

TEMPERATURE: 79–90°F

79°F
▼
90°F

BREEDING STRATEGY: Live-bearer

FOOD: Carnivore

This large, predatory live-bearer can be kept only with fish of like size, especially as older specimens can become quite aggressive. An aquarium planted with *Vallisneria gigantea* and other plants suited to hard water, to which a small amount of salt may be added, and decorated with wood or roots provides the type of environment suited to the lurking and hunting habits of the species. The fish will wait in the shelter of plants and roots before lunging at unsuspecting prey. They are not always on target, and the prey frequently escapes. Piketop Live-bearers will take live fish as well.

Use a large aquarium for breeding, and add salt to the water. A full-grown female may produce 100 or so live young, each about 1in long, and these feed avidly on smaller fish and other live foods. In good conditions, they grow rapidly. The mother does not usually attempt to eat the young.

POECILIA NIGROFASCIATA
(REGAN, 1913)

FAMILY: Poeciliidae

COMMON NAME: Black-barred Limia, Humpbacked Limia

DISTRIBUTION: Haiti

SIZE: Males 1¾in; females 3in

COMPATIBILITY: Peaceful

pH: 7.0–8.5

dH: 10–25°

TEMPERATURE: 72–80°F

BREEDING STRATEGY: Live-bearer

FOOD: Herbivore

7·0
▼
8·5 pH

72°F
▼
80°F

This is an interesting live-bearer for a hard-water or brackish water aquarium, but if you have soft water, do not attempt to keep it. It is peaceful and prefers a planted tank – use *Vallisneria*, Java Fern or any other plant that is tolerant of the conditions the fish demands.

P. nigrofasciata is a herbivore, so if enough algae cannot be produced, supplement the diet with peas, lettuce, spinach and so forth. It will also take flakes and live foods, such as *Daphnia*.

Males are more colorful than females, and their anal fin is modified into a gonopodium. Males also have an arched back, the degree of which increases with age. Females produce 20–30 fry at a time. Remove the female after she has given birth, as she will often eat her own fry.

POECILIA RETICULATA
[PETERS, 1859]

FAMILY: Poeciliidae

COMMON NAME: Guppy

DISTRIBUTION: Central America to Brazil

SIZE: 2½in

COMPATIBILITY: Peaceful

pH: 7.0–8.5

dH: 12–30°

TEMPERATURE: 66–80°F

BREEDING STRATEGY: Live-bearer

FOOD: Omnivore

7·0
▼
8·5 pH

66°F
▼
80°F

Guppies have been kept in aquaria for many years. Their ability to reproduce quickly has made them a favorite among aquarists and commercial breeders, and new fin shapes and colors have been developed. There are some 12 or so recognized tail shapes, ranging from round tails to double sword tails and veil tails. These fish are line bred and displayed at international Guppy shows.

For the average aquarist, they provide color and movement and a chance to breed your first fish. Provided there is plenty of cover, such as clumps of fine-leaved plants and floating plants, the fry will survive in the community aquarium. A good female will produce 20–30 young at a time, and the fry reach maturity in about 12 weeks.

Feeding is simple, but they do have a particular liking for mosquito larvae. This has been put to good use, for in poorly developed countries where malaria is rife, Guppies have been introduced to eat the mosquito larvae.

XIPHOPHORUS HELLERI
HECKEL, 1848

FAMILY: Poeciliidae

COMMON NAME: Swordtail

DISTRIBUTION: Central America

SIZE: Males 4in; females 4¾in

COMPATIBILITY: Peaceful

pH: 7.0–8.5

dH: to 30°

TEMPERATURE: 68–80°F

BREEDING STRATEGY: Live-bearer

FOOD: Omnivore

7·0
▼
8·5 pH

68°F
▼
80°F

This large live-bearer is well suited to a community aquarium. Although males can sometimes be belligerent, it is usually only toward other males of their own kind. If there is plenty of plant cover, some fry will survive, even in a community aquarium. They are no problem to feed: use flakes as a staple and supplement with live foods and green foods.

Adult males are easily distinguished by their gonopodia and sword-like extensions to the lower part of the caudal fins. Females have normal shaped fins, and when they are about to give birth, they show a gravid patch (black area) just in front of their vent. The fish grow a little large to be placed in the average breeding trap to give birth. It is far better to put the gravid females in a separate aquarium with plenty of plant cover.

Over the years, so many color forms have been developed that the Swordtails offered for sale today bear little resemblance to their wild ancestors. Not satisfied with manipulating the fish for color forms, breeders have also played about with the finnage so that forms with double swords and extended finnage can be found.

XIPHOPHORUS MACULATUS
(GUENTHER, 1866)

FAMILY: Poeciliidae

COMMON NAME: Platy

DISTRIBUTION: Mexico, Guatemala, Honduras

SIZE: Male 1¼in; female 2½in

COMPATIBILITY: Peaceful

pH: 7.0–8.2

dH: 10–25°

TEMPERATURE: 66–77°F

BREEDING STRATEGY: Live-bearer

FOOD: Omnivore

7·0
▼
8·2 pH

66°F
▼
77°F

Platies are probably one of the first fish people consider buying. They have been bred to enhance their colors and to develop new color patterns and extended finnage, and it is now possible to buy red, blue, black and yellow platies as well as all the color combinations in between.

They can be kept with most other community fish and will even produce young in the community aquarium. Furnish the tank with *Vallisneria*, Amazon Swords and Java Moss (this will afford cover for the fry). They are omnivorous and have a liking for algae, and for this reason they are often used to help control algal blooms in newly set-up aquaria.

Platies are live-bearers. The anal fin of the male is modified into a copulatory organ known as a gonopodium. Females have normally shaped anal fins. Platies can breed at an early age – 12–16 weeks is usual – so a tank can soon become overpopulated. If you wish to grow the fry on, you will have to get another tank to raise them.

CICHLIDS

This diverse group of fish is found in all but the southern-most regions of South America, north through Central America to Texas in North America. They also occur in Africa, Asia and Madagascar as well as the coastal areas of India and Sri Lanka. In many countries they form an important food source, so that Tilapia species are farmed worldwide in the tropics, and escapees and introductions have wreaked havoc with the native fish fauna.

The body form of cichlids varies greatly from the elongate Pike Cichlids to the laterally compressed Discus and Angelfish. The body and most of the head of cichlids are covered with scales. The lateral line is broken into two parts. Their dorsal and anal fins have a series of spines in the first part of the fin, and thereafter it continues with soft rays. Cichlids have a single nostril on each side of the head.

Because of the great diversity in the family, aquarists often specialize in one type of cichlid, such as those from the Rift Lakes which require hard alkaline waters, or the more delicate West African species which require soft acid waters.

In the main cichlids are colorful, easy to keep and easy to breed, thus making them highly desirable as aquarium fish.

CICHLASOMA SYNSPILUM
HUBBS, 1935

FAMILY: Cichlidae

COMMON NAME: Quetzal

DISTRIBUTION: Guatemala, Belize

SIZE: 12in

COMPATIBILITY: Adults can be pugnacious

pH: 7.0–7.5

dH: 10-15°

TEMPERATURE: 73–80°F

BREEDING STRATEGY: Egg-layer

FOOD: Omnivore

7·0
▼
7·5 pH

73°F
▼
80°F

Juvenile specimens have pretty nondescript coloration, being mainly silver-gray flecked with black and with a crude lateral band. When the fish matures, however, its colors are spectacular. While much of the body remains flecked with black, the lateral line breaks up, the head turns a vivid red, the dorsal surface is tinged with gold contrasting with the bluish hue of the ventral half. This coloration does not appear until the fish is about 8in long.

Sexing is not easy, because there are no visible indicators. The best method of determining sex is by examining the genital papillae, a method used with other Cichlasoma, but the size of the adult fish makes this a hazardous procedure. It is far better to allow a small group of fish to determine their own pairing.

C. synspilum is a substrate spawner and like many other cichlids exercises parental care of both eggs and fry. Be warned though: spawnings can be on the large scale with 1,000 or more eggs being laid.

ETROPLUS MACULATUS
(BLOCH, 1795)

FAMILY: Cichlidae

COMMON NAME: Orange Chromide

DISTRIBUTION: Western India, Sri Lanka

SIZE: 3¼in

COMPATIBILITY: Peaceful

pH: 7.0–8.0

dH: to 25°

7·0
▼
8·0 pH

TEMPERATURE: 70–75°F

70°F
▼
75°F

BREEDING STRATEGY: Egg-layer

FOOD: Omnivore

In the wild Orange Chromides are found in regions of fresh and brackish water. An aquarium should have a sandy substrate, be well planted and be decorated with wood and smooth pebbles or pieces of slate, which will provide spawning sites for the fish. They require stable water conditions, and the addition of a small amount of salt is beneficial.

These fish adapt well to aquarium conditions and, being omnivorous, will feed on most things, from flake to live foods.

Orange Chromides are excellent parents. It is often a little difficult to tell male from female, but females are usually paler colored and do not have the red edge to the finnage. Both parents take care of the brood. Between 200 and 300 "stemmed" eggs are attached to a rock or piece of wood, and after hatching, the fry are moved to depressions in the substrate and guarded by the parents.

HEROS SEVERUM
HECKEL, 1840

FAMILY: Cichlidae

COMMON NAME: Severum, Banded Cichlid

DISTRIBUTION: Fairly widespread throughout northern South America

SIZE: 8in

COMPATIBILITY: Peaceful if with comparably sized fish

6·2
▼
6·7 pH

pH: 6.2–6.7

dH: 5-10°

73°F
▼
77°F

TEMPERATURE: 73–77°F

BREEDING STRATEGY: Egg-layer

FOOD: Omnivore

Just as the distribution of this species is widespread, so its coloration is very variable, ranging from drab gray with faint banding to highly colored with additional flecks of gold, red and blue. Humans have further increased the colors available through selective breeding, and albino and gold varieties are now available.

Live foods are recommended (insect larvae, shrimp and so on) although the fish can be trained to accept alternative foods (try prawn in moderation), flake and tablet foods.

Despite its size, this species is rather shy and retiring, demanding a quiet tank with abundant vegetation and secluded areas. Breeding is possible, but, perhaps because of their retiring nature, the right aquarium conditions must be provided. Pairing can be a very protracted exercise, with both sexes being choosy about their mate. Adult males are distinguished by extensions to the dorsal and anal fins. The spawning strategy is similar to that of many other cichlids from South and Central America – eggs are laid on a flat, clean surface, and both eggs and fry are protected by the parents.

Sometimes referred to as the Poor Man's Discus, this species is a worthy addition to any collection of American cichlids.

JULIDOCHROMIS MARLIERI
POLL, 1956

FAMILY: Cichlidae

COMMON NAME: Marler's Julie

DISTRIBUTION: Lake Tanganyika

SIZE: 4–5½in

COMPATIBILITY: Intolerant of own species

pH: 7.5–9.0

dH: 12–14°

TEMPERATURE: 72–77°F

BREEDING STRATEGY: Egg-layer

FOOD: Omnivore

7·5
▼
9·0 pH

72°F
▼
77°F

This attractive cichlid is ideal for the smaller aquarium. Furnish the tank with rocks so that there are plenty of caves and places in which the fish can shelter. Plants such as Java Fern may be used, but they are not essential.

Most foods are accepted, but alternate flakes, frozen and live foods to provide a varied diet.

The fish breed in caves. When they are ready to breed, the females may be distinguished by their genital papillae, and they are also slightly larger than the males. Females lay 100–150 eggs, and both parents guard the eggs and resultant fry. The family unit remains intact for quite some time, and the fry may be fed on microworms, brine shrimps or similar small foods.

MELANOCHROMIS AURATUS
(BOULENGER, 1897)

FAMILY: Cichlidae

COMMON NAME: Golden Cichlid

DISTRIBUTION: Lake Malawi

SIZE: 3½in

COMPATIBILITY: Relatively peaceful, but do not keep with very small fish

pH: 7.6–8.2

dH: 10-15°

TEMPERATURE: 72–77°F

BREEDING STRATEGY: Egg-layer

FOOD: Omnivore

7·6
▼
8·2 pH

72°F
▼
77°F

This species was one of the first fish from Lake Malawi to have been introduced into the aquarium hobby. It has a fairly variable coloration, as a result of its widespread distribution in the lake, where it is mainly found on the rocky shores.

It is not as territorial as other African Rift Lake cichlids, but it can become aggressive during breeding. *M. auratus* is fairly easy to breed and fascinating to observe. It is a mouth-brooder – that is, the female incubates the eggs in her mouth. Even after hatching, the fry still seek the safety of the mother's mouth.

NEOLAMPROLOGUS ELONGATUS
(TREWAVAS & POLL, 1952)

FAMILY: Cichlidae

COMMON NAME: Lyre-tailed Neolamprologus

DISTRIBUTION: Lake Tanganyika

SIZE: 4in

COMPATIBILITY: Can be territorial

pH: 7.5–8.2

dH: 10–15°

TEMPERATURE: 73–79°F

BREEDING STRATEGY: Egg-layer

FOOD: Insectivore

7·5
▼
8·2 pH

73°F
▼
79°F

In its natural environment there are many different tribes of *N. elongatus*, each with its own distinct markings. Its natural rocky habitat on the shores of Lake Tanganyika should be simulated in the aquarium.

N. elongatus feeds on copious quantities of small invertebrates such as *Daphnia*, although some specimens can be encouraged to accept flake foods.

Pairing is for life, and the spawning site is similarly retained. *N. elongatus* is a substrate spawner, both parents looking after eggs and fry.

Most of the problems encountered in keeping this species are generally related to the condition of the water, which must always be alkaline and moderately hard.

PSEUDOCRENILABRUS PHILANDER PHILANDER
(WEBER, 1897)

FAMILY: Cichlidae

DISTRIBUTION: Southwest and Central Africa

SIZE: 3½in

COMPATIBILITY: Can be aggressive; keep with other fish of similar size

pH: Neutral – 7

dH: 10-15°

TEMPERATURE: 72–77°F

BREEDING STRATEGY: Egg-layer

FOOD: Omnivore

Neutral
▼
7·0 pH

72°F
▼
77°F

This rather attractive fish thrives in a community aquarium with abundant plant growth, as long as the other fish are carefully selected. The intensity of the color may be enhanced through diet – abundant insect larvae, such as bloodworms or mosquito, for example – and by keeping both male and females together, which will encourage the male to display frequently. This cichlid will accept dried foods, although insect larvae are ideal for conditioning.

This fish is a mouth-brooder which will readily breed in a well-planted aquarium. The eggs are laid in a shallow depression in the substrate, but the female will then pick them up in her mouth, where they remain until they hatch. It is advisable to remove the male at this stage in case he becomes too belligerent with the female. The young hatch in 8–10 days, but even then are still tended buccally by the female, the fry making only brief excursions outside the confines of their mother's mouth. During this period the female can become quite emaciated, but the temporary fasting lasts only until the fry are considered large enough to be left unattended for longer periods.

PTEROPHYLLUM SCALARE
(LICHTENSTEIN, 1823)

FAMILY: Cichlidae

COMMON NAME: Angelfish

DISTRIBUTION: Widespread in tropical South America

SIZE: 4in

COMPATIBILITY: Peaceful, but will eat small fry of other fish

6·5 ▼ 7·0 pH

pH: 6.5–7.0

dH: 5–12°

75°F ▼ 80°F

TEMPERATURE: 75–80°F

BREEDING STRATEGY: Egg-layer

FOOD: Omnivore

This cichlid lacks the pugnaciousness of other fish in the same family, and it is often an aquarist's first experience with keeping cichlids.

The specimen illustrated here is the natural color form, but selective breeding has given rise to many varieties, both in markings and finnage. The species' main requirements are a well-planted and preferably fairly deep tank to accommodate the extraordinary depth of the Angelfish. The other inmates should not be dither fish, and certainly not species with reputations for fin nipping. Feed with both prepared aquarium flaked foods and live foods, such as mosquito and gnat larvae.

They are best kept as a small school rather than singly, so that they can form their own pairings, which are often for life. The breeding site is usually a broad-leafed plant, such as the Amazon Sword, and the eggs are laid on a leaf. Both eggs and freshly hatched fry are attended by both parents. The fry require small live foods, such as brine shrimp.

STEATOCRANUS CASUARIUS
POLL, 1939

FAMILY: Cichlidae ·

COMMON NAME: Blockhead Cichlid, African Blockhead

DISTRIBUTION: Lower and central Zaire

SIZE: 3¼–4in

COMPATIBILITY: Belligerent, particularly during breeding; best kept with fish of similar disposition, but not in too crowded conditions

6·5 ▼ 7·0 pH

pH: 6.5–7.0

dH: 12-18°

75°F ▼ 80°F

TEMPERATURE: 75–80°F

BREEDING STRATEGY: Egg-layer

FOOD: Omnivore

The natural habitat of this species is fast-flowing, well-oxygenated water with a rocky substrate. The common name, Blockhead, refers to the cranial hump, which is particularly pronounced on males. The fish move not by normal swimming movements, but by "hopping" from one settling place to another, in a similar fashion to many gobies.

This cichlid will accept prepared aquarium food, but prefers live foods.

S. casuarius is monogamous, and the pairing is often for life. In the aquarium the fish spawn in a cave or upturned clay flowerpot, after they have cleaned the substrate and dug a slight depression within the cave. Both male and female tend the eggs and fry at different stages of development, although feeding is normally conducted by the female.

SYMPHYSODON DISCUS
HECKEL, 1840

FAMILY: Cichlidae

COMMON NAME: Discus, Pompadour

DISTRIBUTION: Brazilian Amazon

SIZE: 8in

COMPATIBILITY: Peaceful but best kept in isolation of other species

pH: 6.0–6.5

6·0
▼
6·5 pH

dH: 2–5°

TEMPERATURE: 77–84°F

77°F
▼
84°F

BREEDING STRATEGY: Egg-layer

FOOD: Insectivore

Long regarded as the monarchs of freshwater fish, adult Discus make a superb aquarium display.

Adults, which are the size of a dinner plate, have striking coloration and majestic deportment. However, to achieve this, a considerable amount of attention must be paid to the water chemistry and temperature. Filtration and water quality are also important: slow, gentle water movement is essential. They are rather retiring fish, demanding low levels of activity both within and in the vicinity of the aquarium. As a result, many aquarists keep this fish in isolation with perhaps only one pair to a tank. Feed on small aquatic invertebrates, insect larvae and so on.

There are two species of Discus, *S. discus* and *S. aequifasciata*, with a number of subspecies. Color forms are diverse, largely because of selective breeding, and there are now more than 100 recognized color forms of the two species.

Breeding is possible only if strict attention is paid to the water conditions. Eggs are laid on a firm, vertical surface, which the parents will have pre-cleaned. Both sexes tend to the eggs. The fry initially feed from the mucus on the parents' bodies, and it is important, therefore, that at this early stage the fry are not separated from their parents. After a few days, brine shrimp should be offered to the fry.

THORICHTHYS MEEKI
(BRIND, 1918)

FAMILY: Cichlidae

COMMON NAME: Firemouth Cichlid

DISTRIBUTION: Guatemala, Yucatan, Mexico

SIZE: 6in

COMPATIBILITY: Suitable only with fish of similar size; can be aggressive, particularly when breeding

6·7
▼
7·0 pH

pH: 6.7–7.0

dH: 8-12°

70°F
▼
77°F

TEMPERATURE: 70–77°F

BREEDING STRATEGY: Egg-layer

FOOD: Carnivore

The common name, Firemouth, alludes to the flame-red coloration on the ventral surface, especially on the underside of the head and on the operculum, or gill cover. There is also a black spot ringed with gold on the operculum which, when the gill cover is outspread, mimics the eyes of a much larger fish. The red coloration is more apparent on the males, who, with the operculum spread out, use it as a threat posture to ward off unwanted intruders to their territories. They also use it effectively in breeding displays.

Food is live foods (including small fish, should the opportunity arise), but it will accept flake and tablet foods.

These are fairly easy fish to spawn in captivity, although best results will be achieved in isolation of other fish to avoid over aggressive behavioral problems. Up to 400 eggs are laid on a precleaned rocky substrate and tended by both parents. After the young hatch, the parents dig pits in the gravel, in which they guard the fry. After the first spawning, subsequent spawnings will occur at regular intervals. The fry are best fed on brine shrimp nauplii.

Many of the specimens now available to aquarists are captive-bred rather than wild-caught, and they often lack the color intensity and size of the naturally occurring fish.

LABYRINTH FISH

These fish are also referred to as Anabantids, Gouramis and Climbing Perch. At first glance, these fish could be mistaken for perch as the first part of their dorsal and anal fins are composed of spines followed by a series of soft rays. But the most notable difference is the possession of a labyrinth organ. This accessory breathing mechanism is found just above the gills in each gill chamber and allows the fish to utilize atmospheric air. These fish are often found in stagnant or semi-stagnant water or water that is very warm and thus low in oxygen. The need to breathe air, therefore, is paramount to their survival: if a labyrinth fish is prevented from reaching the water's surface, it can perish.

These fish also produce bubble-nests, another adaptation to a harsh environment. This type of nest keeps the eggs in an oxygen-rich environment which is necessary for their development.

Betta splendens, *the Siamese Fighter, has been bred to enhance its finnage so that today's males have greatly elongated fins when compared with their wild counterparts. Other species, such as the Dwarf Gourami and the Blue Gourami, have also been bred commercially to enhance different colors or body patterns.*

BELONTIA SIGNATA
(GUENTHER, 1861)

FAMILY: Belontiidae

COMMON NAME: Combtail

DISTRIBUTION: Sri Lanka

SIZE: 5in

COMPATIBILITY: Boisterous, can fin nip

pH: 6.5–7.5

6·5 ▼ 7·5 pH

dH: 10–20°

TEMPERATURE: 75–82°F

75°F ▼ 82°F

BREEDING STRATEGY: Egg-layer

FOOD: Omnivore

Combtails have a bad reputation among aquarists, for they are boisterous, very aggressive when breeding, and may nip fins. For all their faults, however, they deserve a chance.

The aquarium should be well-furnished with plants and hiding places. Use some broad-leaved plants, such as *Cryptocoryne* species, Amazon Swordplants, and if you are intending to try to breed them, include some fine-leaved species such as *Hygrophila arcuata* and Java Moss. Feeding presents no problems. Combtails eat anything and everything they can fit into their mouths.

Males may be distinguished by their extended dorsal fins. In the courtship display there is much spreading of fins and the colors intensify. The eggs are laid in an air bubble (not a frothy bubble nest) in clumps under plant leaves. The fry hatch in five to seven days and will immediately feed on newly hatched brine shrimp, crumbled flake food and fine *Daphnia*. If there are sufficient hiding places – clumps of fine-leaved plants, for example – the fry can be raised with the parents, but do not expect a 100 percent survival rate using this method because feeding the young can be difficult and you have to put large amounts of food into the tank to make sure that the youngsters get enough.

BETTA SPLENDENS
REGAN, 1910

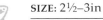

FAMILY: Belontiidae

COMMON NAME: Siamese Fighter, Siamese Fighting Fish

DISTRIBUTION: Thailand, Cambodia

SIZE: 2½–3in

COMPATIBILITY: Usually peaceful but can be aggressive toward smaller fish

6·0
▼
8·0 pH

pH: 6.0–8.0

dH: to 25°

75°F
▼
86°F

TEMPERATURE: 75–86°F

BREEDING STRATEGY: Egg-layer, bubble-nest builder

FOOD: Insectivore

The history of this fish as a pugilist is well known. In the countries of origin, males are pitted against each other, and during the fights they posture and flare their gill covers before lunging to tear the other fish's fins to shreds. It is not possible to keep more than one male in the aquarium.

To keep them at their best, provide high temperatures and slow water movement. For breeding, the water should be shallow – only about 10in deep. Keep them well fed on live and flake foods, and they will breed. One male to about three females seems to be the best ratio. The male blows bubbles into plants until a foamy mass rises to the surface of the water. He then courts his chosen female, displaying with fins spread and shimmying, until they are beneath the nest and she submits to his advances. He wraps his body around her, and the eggs and milt are released. The fry hatch in 24 hours. When they are small, they require infusoria, very finely crushed flake food or newly hatched brine shrimp. For the first few days, the male guards the nest, catching and blowing back any eggs or fry that fall from it. He will chase the female away, and, if the aquarium is small, she should be removed.

COLISA CHUNA
(HAMILTON, 1822)

FAMILY: Belontiidae

COMMON NAME: Honey Gourami

DISTRIBUTION: Northeast India, Assam, Bangladesh

SIZE: 2in

COMPATIBILITY: Peaceful

6·0
▼
7·5 pH

pH: 6.0–7.5

dH: to 15°

72°F
▼
82°F

TEMPERATURE: 72–82°F

BREEDING STRATEGY: Egg-layer, bubble-nest builder

FOOD: Insectivore

This delicate little gourami is often overlooked because of its juvenile coloration. Immature males and females are a drab, gray-brown color with a longitudinal brown stripe. It is not until they are some 1¼–1½in long that the males develop the wonderful orange-brown body and the almost navy blue band that runs from below the snout along the belly to the anal fin. The dorsal fin becomes edged with yellow. The females remain silvery brown with the longitudinal brown stripe.

All forms of small live foods are avidly consumed, and these are almost essential to bring them into peak condition for spawning. Flake foods are also taken.

It is possible to breed Honey Gouramis, but it can be difficult to raise the fry. Raise the temperature of the water to 79–82°F. The male constructs a small bubble nest among floating vegetation. As he courts the female, his colors intensify. When she submits, the spawning embrace occurs beneath the nest, and the eggs and milt are released and float up into the bubbles. The male guards the nest until the fry are free swimming, gently catching and blowing back into the nest any eggs or fry that fall from it. First foods are infusoria followed by brine shrimp nauplii.

COLISA LALIA
(HAMILTON, 1822)

FAMILY: Belontiidae

COMMON NAME: Dwarf Gourami

DISTRIBUTION: Northeast India, Assam, Bangladesh

SIZE: 2in

COMPATIBILITY: Peaceful

6·0
▼
7·5 pH

pH: 6.0–7.5

dH: to 15°

75°F
▼
82°F

TEMPERATURE: 75–82°F

BREEDING STRATEGY: Egg-layer, bubble-nest builder

FOOD: Insectivore

The Dwarf Gourami has long been a favorite among aquarists, and in response to this demand fish breeders in the Far East and Florida have developed several color forms, including red, royal blue and sunset, and also a long-finned variety.

The species is very attractively colored. Red and blue vertical stripes adorn the flanks and extend into the finnage of male fish, and the throat region is electric blue. Females are drab by comparison, with only a few vertical blue bars apparent on a silvery gold background.

Dwarf Gouramis are easy to breed and will often do so in the community aquarium, although under these circumstances the survival rate of the fry is very low. The male constructs a large bubble nest and incorporates vast amounts of plant material. He guards the eggs and fry until they are free swimming.

Adults thrive on a diet of live foods and good-quality flaked foods. First foods for the fry are infusoria followed by newly hatched brine shrimp and, later, *Daphnia*, and a variety of small frozen and dried foods.

CTENOPOMA ACUTIROSTRE
PELLEGRIN, 1899

FAMILY: Anabantidae

COMMON NAME: Spotted Climbing Perch

DISTRIBUTION: Zaire

SIZE: 4–6in

COMPATIBILITY: Peaceful, somewhat timid

pH: 6.5–7.0

6·5
▼
7·0 pH

dH: 3–12°

TEMPERATURE: 73–82°F

73°F
▼
82°F

BREEDING STRATEGY: Egg-layer, bubble-nest builder

FOOD: Insectivore

C. acutirostre tends to spend most of its time in the lower levels of the aquarium. Its coloration – dark brown spots over a beige/light brown background – allows it to blend in well with plants and roots. It can be very timid, so the aquarium should be well planted but with some open swimming areas and not too brightly lit. Avoid very boisterous companions.

Although youngsters can be difficult to feed, taking only live foods in the first instance, they are well worth the bother of keeping. Once they are settled in the aquarium, they will take flake and tablet foods if they have to and frozen foods with a little more relish. However, they prefer live food, and when they are stalking larger insect larvae they are particularly impressive, drifting, almost leaf-like, up to the prey, their fins spread and the color intensifying. A lunge to capture it, and the fish retires to a quiet area to eat its meal.

These fish have been bred in captivity. They build a bubble nest, so it is essential to provide some vegetation that reaches the surface of the water because the nest will be placed in a quiet area of the tank among the plants or perhaps beneath a floating leaf. The water must be very soft (2–5°), with the pH in the range quoted above. Water temperature should be at the higher end of the range, about 79–82°F. First foods for the fry should be infusoria or the smallest brine shrimp nauplii.

HELOSTOMA TEMMINCKII
CUVIER & VALENCIENNES, 1831

FAMILY: Helostomatidae

COMMON NAME: Kissing Gourami

DISTRIBUTION: Green form, Thailand; pink form, Java

SIZE: 2½–4in

COMPATIBILITY: Peaceful

pH: 6.8–8.5

dH: to 30°

TEMPERATURE: 72–80°F

BREEDING STRATEGY: Egg-layer

FOOD: Herbivore

6·8 ▼ 8·5 pH

72°F ▼ 80°F

Kissing Gouramis are great favorites for the aquarium because of the males' habit of fighting by pressing their mouths together, which is the origin of their common name. These are trials of strength, and the weaker fish soon gives in.

They require an aquarium with plenty of swimming space. Furnish it with robust plants such as large Amazon Swords, Java Fern and Java Moss, for they will eat most vegetation. Kissing Gouramis, are, in fact, often used by aquarists to control algae, especially in newly set up tanks, and you should keep the front glass clean, but leave some algae on the other faces for the fish to graze on. In addition, they can be fed lettuce and peas, and if enough of this greenstuff is offered, they will leave the aquarium plants alone. They appreciate some live foods, such as *Daphnia*, and will also take flake foods. These fish supplement their diet by filtering plankton through their gills.

It is difficult to distinguish the sexes. They do not build a nest, but the eggs float. Provide some lettuce leaves, which will float on the water's surface and slowly decompose, so producing bacteria and infusoria for the fry to feed on.

SPHAERICHTHYS OSPHROMENOIDES
CANESTRINI, 1860

FAMILY: Belontiidae

COMMON NAME: Chocolate Gourami

DISTRIBUTION: Sumatra, Borneo, Malaysia

SIZE: 2in

COMPATIBILITY: Peaceful

pH: 6.0–7.0

dH: 2–4°

TEMPERATURE: 73–86°F

BREEDING STRATEGY: Mouth-brooder

FOOD: Insectivore

6·0 ▼ 7·0 pH

73°F ▼ 86°F

This is a fish with a reputation for being difficult, and it is really suited to the more experienced aquarist who is looking for a challenge. The key to success lies in the provision of excellent water conditions. The fish require a mature aquarium – one that has been running for 12 months or more – and it should be well planted. Companion fishes should not be too boisterous. Success seems more likely when the fish are kept in a school of about 10 in a 50 × 20 × 20in furnished aquarium with soft (4°dH), acidic (pH 6–6.6) water at a temperature of 72–73°F, and allowed to pair themselves. Although most books recommend that spawning pairs be kept, the above method has been proved to work.

Offer these fish copious amounts of live food. They will also accept flake and frozen foods, such as bloodworm, *Mysis* shrimp and *Daphnia*.

Males are slimmer than females, and they have a yellow edge to their dorsal and anal fins. When they are spawning, the fish become very dark, almost navy blue in color, and the yellow intensifies. The eggs are deposited on the substrate, fertilized by the male, and picked up by the female. She incubates an average of 30 eggs for about 14 days, during which time she does not feed. Because of this, it is absolutely essential that the fish are as fit as possible before attempting to spawn them. First foods for the fry are brine shrimp and other small live foods.

TRICHOGASTER LEERI
(BLEEKER, 1852)

FAMILY: Belontiidae

COMMON NAME: Pearl Gourami, Leeri

DISTRIBUTION: Sumatra, Malaysia, Borneo

SIZE: 4¾in

COMPATIBILITY: Peaceful

pH: 6.5–8.5

6·5
▼
8·5 pH

dH: to 30°

TEMPERATURE: 75–82°F

75°F
▼
82°F

BREEDING STRATEGY: Egg-layer, bubble-nest builder

FOOD: Omnivore

This medium-sized anabantid is one of the most peaceful fishes available. Their finnage and coloration, especially at breeding time, are spectacular. The male has an extended dorsal fin and elongated rays on the anal fin, while the throat and chest become an intense orange and the white spots on the body almost shine from the dark background. The female lacks the fin extensions and the throat color, but still displays the lacelike patterning over the body and fins.

In the wild they are found in rivers and streams that have a dense plant growth, and in the aquarium they are at their best when there is plenty of plant cover. Their companions should be peaceful, as any aggressive fish will be tempted to attack and nip at the extended finnage of the males.

These creatures will breed quite readily if the water level is dropped to about 4¾in. Maintain the humidity above the water by using a tight-fitting cover glass. They will choose a heavily planted area, and the male will blow a large nest in among the plants. If a floating plant such as *Riccia fluitans* is available, this will be incorporated in to the nest. The male guards the nest after spawning until the fry become free-swimming. First foods are newly hatched brine shrimp, very fine *Daphnia* and crushed flakes.

TRICHOGASTER TRICHOPTERUS
(PALLAS, 1777)

FAMILY: Belontiidae

COMMON NAME: Three-spot Gourami, Blue Gourami

DISTRIBUTION: Malaysia, Thailand, Burma, Vietnam

SIZE: 4in

COMPATIBILITY: Peaceful, although two males may fight

6·0
▼
8·5 pH

pH: 6.0–8.5

75°F
▼
82°F

dH: to 35°

TEMPERATURE: 75–82°F

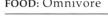

BREEDING STRATEGY: Egg-layer, bubble-nest builder

FOOD: Omnivore

This is perhaps the most hardy of the gouramis and is an ideal fish for the beginner because it will tolerate most water conditions, will accept most foods, and will breed readily. Tank mates should not be too boisterous, or the Blue Gourami will retire to a quiet corner of the aquarium.

Feeding is simplicity itself, for these fish will eat almost anything, from flakes to dried insect larvae, from oatmeal to chopped pieces of meat, and from frozen foods to live foods.

For breeding, the water level should be reduced to about 6in. Make sure that the air above the water is kept hot and humid by using a tight glass cover on the aquarium. This is important so that the fry do not become chilled and die when they rise to the surface to take their first gulps of air. The male constructs quite a large bubble nest, and he chases the female hard prior and during spawning. The colors of the fish intensify to such a degree that they may become almost navy blue. The spawning embrace takes place below the nest. Once spawning is completed, the male drives off the female and stands guard over the nest, repairing it as necessary until the fry are free-swimming. Remove the female after spawning because the male can become very aggressive while guarding his offspring. First foods are newly hatched brine shrimp and fine flake.

CATFISH

The *Siluriformes*, or *catfish, are a very diverse group, both in habitat and body form. They are found worldwide with the exception of the polar regions. They inhabit every conceivable habitat from clear, cool mountain torrents to hot, almost stagnant pools, from soft acid waters to brackish and marine environments.*

Catfish do not have scales. Some, such as the bagrids, are naked, their bodies covered with a thick skin; others, such as the loricariids, have their bodies covered in bony plates. All catfish have highly sensory barbels, and all possess the Weberian Apparatus. The first dorsal and pectoral fins have a fin spine which may or may not be serrated and, in some cases, is thickened to produce quite a pungent spine. These can be locked out to increase the fish's effective body area or locked into position to hold them in crevices.

Catfish can also produce sound either by stridulation – moving their fin spines so that the articulating surfaces rub together – or by vibrating their swim bladder using the elastic spring mechanism.

Many species are now being bred by aquarists and commercially for the aquarium trade and as food fish.

BROCHIS SPLENDENS
(CASTELNAU, 1855)

FAMILY: Callichthyidae

COMMON NAME: Young fish are sometimes sold as Sailfin Corydoras

DISTRIBUTION: Widespread throughout Peru, Ecuador, Brazil

SIZE: 3–3¼in

COMPATIBILITY: Peaceful, community

pH: 6.0–8.0

dH: 2–30°

TEMPERATURE: 72–80°F

BREEDING STRATEGY: Egg-layer

FOOD: Insectivore

6·0 ▼ 8·0 pH

72°F ▼ 80°F

Young *B. splendens* are particularly attractive as they have high, strikingly colored sailfin dorsals with a white margin. As the fish grows, the dorsal fin loses the intensity of color, and the size becomes more in proportion to the body. They are active during the day, and a group of five or six makes a welcome addition to the community aquarium. Feeding is simple: they will take flake and tablet foods. However, if the iridescent green sheen is to be maintained on the body, it is essential to supplement the diet with copious amounts of live foods such as *Daphnia*, mosquito larvae and well-cleaned *Tubifex*.

Breeding has been achieved in captivity. Between 100 and 200 light yellow eggs are laid near the water surface. The eggs are attached individually to the undersides of floating water plant leaves or on the glass of the aquarium. They hatch after four days at a temperature of 73°F, and the fry are about ¼in long. After absorption of the yolk sac, they will accept brine shrimp. By 12 days old, they will have doubled their size and developed the sail-like dorsal fin.

Because these fish dig for food in the substrate, it is important that the gravel is not sharp; better still, use sand with well-rounded particles.

There are two other species of *Brochis*, *B. multiradiatus* (Orcés-Villaggomez, 1960), which is distinguished from *B. splendens* by having 17 dorsal fin rays, and *B. britskii* Nijssen & Isbrücker, 1983, which is similar to *B. multiradiatus*, but has a shorter snout.

CORYDORAS PALEATUS
(JENYNS, 1842)

FAMILY: Callichthyidae

COMMON NAME: Peppered Corydoras

DISTRIBUTION: La Plata river system, southeastern Brazil

SIZE: male 2¾in; female 3¼in

COMPATIBILITY: Peaceful, community

pH: 6.5–7.5

6·5
▼
7·5 pH

dH: 6–15°

TEMPERATURE: 72–77°F

72°F
▼
77°F

BREEDING STRATEGY: Egg-layer

FOOD: Insectivore

C. paleatus is probably one of the most commonly available species of *Corydoras*, and it is bred commercially in Florida and in the Far East. It adapts well to aquarium conditions, doing best when kept in groups of between three and six specimens. Feeding is simple – offer a good quality flake or pelleted food and supplement these with live or frozen *Daphnia* and bloodworms. Wild specimens are occasionally imported, and these are more demanding in their requirements. Because of the widespread distribution of the species, the coloration and finnage length can differ from population to population.

Breeding in the aquarium is possible, and, in fact, this fish was first spawned in France as long ago as 1878. Males are generally smaller and slimmer than females. Eggs are normally deposited on leaves, the aquarium glass, or other surface.

EUTROPIELLUS DEBAUWI
(BOULENGER, 1900)

FAMILY: Schilbeidae

COMMON NAME: African Glass Catfish

DISTRIBUTION: Zaire, Gabon

SIZE: 3¼in

COMPATIBILITY: Peaceful, community

pH: 6.0–7.5

6·0
▼
7·5 pH

dH: 6–20°

TEMPERATURE: 72–79°F

72°F
▼
79°F

BREEDING STRATEGY: Egg scatterer

FOOD: Insectivore

This school catfish must be kept in a group of six or more if it is to thrive. The aquarium should be planted but have plenty of open water, as these fish are very active. They will accept most water conditions, but they do require it to be clean, mature, well filtered, and with a reasonable current such as that provided by an external power filter. When they are not cruising around the aquarium, they can usually be found resting in the shelter of plants, hanging tail down in mid-water. It can sometimes be difficult to acclimatize the African Glass Catfish to aquarium conditions, and if the water is too new or if the filtration system is not working to peak efficiency, the fish will become stressed and will be lethargic and susceptible to all manner of diseases, including white spot, fungus and fin rot.

It is not possible to tell young male from female fish, but, as they grow, females become deeper-bodied and lighter colored than males of similar length.

Feeding is not a problem. They accept anything and everything. However, if you wish to try and breed them, live foods are an essential part of their diet, and frozen foods may also be offered.

HEMISYNODONTIS MEMBRANACEUS
(GEOFFREY-ST HILAIRE, 1809)

FAMILY: Mochokidae

DISTRIBUTION: Widespread throughout the Nile Valley; West Africa from the Gambia and Senegal basins through the Volta and Niger basins to the Chad basin in Central Africa

SIZE: 19in

COMPATIBILITY: Peaceful among like-sized, quiet fish

6·8 ▼ 7·2 pH

pH: 6.8–7.2

dH: to 25°

72°F ▼ 77°F

TEMPERATURE: 72–77°F

BREEDING STRATEGY: Unknown

FOOD: Plankton and small invertebrates

There is little to differentiate this dark gray mochokid from any other dark gray mochokid until you look at the barbels. Mochokids have three pairs of barbels, one maxillary pair and two branched mandibular pairs. *H. membranaceus* has modified maxillary barbels. There is a wide black membrane along their entire length, and it is not until you see them feeding that its function becomes apparent. *H. membranaceus* is one of the few mochokids that inverts to feed and, when it does so, it spreads its barbels and the membrane forms a funnel down which the plankton and other microorganisms are channeled. The food-laden water passes into the mouth and over the gill rakers, where the edible material is filtered out.

Because this is a naked catfish – i.e., its body is not covered by scales or plates – you must make sure that there are no sharp rocks or splinters of wood in the aquarium, as any slight scratch will show on the body. Floating plants or a piece of cork bark will give the fish a degree of security, and it will often rest beneath this and dart out to feed. Make sure that copious amounts of live food such as *Daphnia* are offered.

HYPOPTOPOMA INEXPECTATUM
(HOLMBERG, 1893)

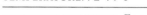

FAMILY: Loricariidae

DISTRIBUTION: Rio Paraguay, South America

SIZE: 3¼in standard length

COMPATIBILITY: Peaceful, suitable for the community tank

6·2 ▼ 7·5 pH

pH: 6.2–7.5

dH: 5–15°

TEMPERATURE: 72–79°F

72°F ▼ 79°F

BREEDING STRATEGY: Egg-layer

FOOD: Herbivore

Although it is somewhat similar in appearance to *Otocinclus paulinus*, this fish is shy, preferring the security of dark areas in the aquarium. It is also more solitary in its lifestyle, rarely interacting with others of its own species. One principal difference between the two species is the position of the eyes, which are more laterally placed on *Hypoptopoma*.

If there is insufficient algal growth on which *H. inexpectatum* feeds, lettuce leaves or frozen peas may be offered as well.

The bony plates that encase this species are covered with fine, hair-like denticles, which give it a rather coarse, sandpaper-like texture. Take care when you net this fish because the net may become entangled with both the fin spines and the body denticles.

The precise breeding strategy is unknown.

OTOCINCLUS PAULINUS
REGAN, 1904

FAMILY: Loricariidae

DISTRIBUTION: Rio Piracicaba, near São Paulo in southern Brazil

SIZE: 1½in

COMPATIBILITY: Peaceful with smallest of fish; ideal community tank inmate

pH: 6.5–7.2

dH: 8–20°

TEMPERATURE: 72–77°F

BREEDING STRATEGY: Egg-layer

FOOD: Principally herbivore

6·5
▼
7·2 pH

72°F
▼
79°F

This diminutive catfish belongs to a large and diverse family of South American catfish, some of which grow to more than 20in. Unlike its close relatives however, *O. paulinus* rarely exceeds 1½in, more usually growing to 1–1¼in.

The small body of *O. paulinus* is virtually enclosed in bony plates. These plates, which are superficially similar to scales, are composed of ossified bone, and they afford the fish

considerable protection from both the harsh environment of swift-flowing water currents and from some predators.

O. paulinus will often be found in the upper reaches of the water column, using its fine teeth and small sucker mouth to graze on the algae growing on the wood and rocks. Here, its brown coloration helps it blend with the substrate on which it is browsing. It is often seen during daylight hours, particularly if kept in groups of six or more. Captive breeding of this species is rare.

PELTEOBAGRUS ORNATUS
(DUNCKER, 1904)

FAMILY: Bagridae

DISTRIBUTION: River Muar, Malaya

SIZE: 1in

COMPATIBILITY: Peaceful, community

pH: 5.0–7.0

dH: 10°

TEMPERATURE: 72–74°F

5·0
▼
7·0 pH

BREEDING STRATEGY: Egg-layer

72°F
▼
74°F

FOOD: Insectivore

This small, delicate catfish has a translucent body with a yellowish sheen – indeed, the dark lateral band on one side of the fish may be seen through the body from the other side. It is best kept in schools of eight or more in a well-planted aquarium. Once settled, it will be seen for most of the day foraging for food or swimming in mid-water.

This can be a difficult fish to acclimatize to aquarium conditions. It requires clean, clear, mature, well-filtered water. Any degradation of water quality results in lethargic fish and the degeneration of fin membranes and barbels. The companion

fish should be equally peaceful, and you should avoid fin nipping species at all costs.

It is possible to distinguish between the sexes. Females are generally more robust than males of the same length, and they have a more rounded profile to the anal fin. In addition, when they are full of roe, the blue-green eggs are clearly visible in the female's body cavity. The eggs are reported to be deposited on plants.

The fish feeds avidly on live small insect larvae, *Daphnia* and the like, which are essential to maintain them in breeding condition. They will also take flake, tablet and frozen foods of suitable size.

PSEUDACANTHICUS SPINOSUS
(DE CASTELNAU, 1855)

FAMILY: Loricariidae

DISTRIBUTION: Amazon River, South America

SIZE: 6in

COMPATIBILITY: Not suited to the community tank

pH: 6.5–7.2

dH: 10–18°

TEMPERATURE: 73–80°F

BREEDING STRATEGY: Egg-layers

FOOD: Herbivore

6·5
▼
7·2 pH

73°F
▼
80°F

In the confines of an aquarium, this sucker-mouthed catfish can, when adult, be rather boisterous and territorial, particularly with others of its own species. Arguments over territory, which can, on occasions, exceed the tank size, lead to fights, particularly between males. This takes the form of butting the opponent and attacking with the extended opercular spines, which are found just behind the gill cover. This behavior means that a large tank must be used if peace is to be maintained, and the fish is best left to the experienced specialist aquarist.

Sexes can be easily identified, both by the more full-bodied form of the females and by the red tint to the leading edge of all the fins on males. (The picture below shows a male.) Precise breeding strategy unknown.

PSEUDACANTHICUS SPINOSUS

SORUBIM LIMA
(BLOCH & SCHNEIDER, 1801)

FAMILY: Pimelodidae

COMMON NAME: Shovelnose Catfish

DISTRIBUTION: Venezuela, Paraguay and the Amazon basin

SIZE: to 2ft

COMPATIBILITY: Peaceful with its own kind and with fish large enough not to be swallowed

pH: 6.5–7.5

dH: up to 20°

TEMPERATURE: 72–76°F

BREEDING STRATEGY: Not known

FOOD: Piscivore

6·5
▼
7·5 pH

72°F
▼
76°F

S. lima is one of the most attractive shovelnose catfish offered for sale. A broad, dark band runs along the flanks, and another band runs along the back. Between them is a marbled pattern over a coppery background. In contrast, the lower body and belly are creamy white. The body is naked, but there are a series of thin dermal plates on the anterior portion of the lateral line. The three pairs of barbels, which are used when hunting, are covered with sensitive taste receptors. The fish can often be seen cruising just above the substrate with the mandibular barbels barely touching it. Should they detect anything edible, the fish will stop, turn, and snap at it.

The aquarium needs to be large – at least $50 \times 20 \times 20$in for small specimens – and the filtration system must be capable of coping with high protein waste. Any deterioration in water quality will result in the degeneration of the fin membranes. Another indicator of stress is the shedding of the body mucus.

Feeding should not be a problem, although you should be prepared to feed live fish if all else fails. Young specimens adapt well to aquarium conditions and can be fed live shrimps and earthworms; later they may be weaned onto dead meaty foods and tablet foods.

SORUBIM LIMA

SYNONDONTIS NIGRIVENTRIS
DAVID, 1936

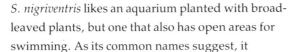

FAMILY: Mochokidae

COMMON NAME: Upside-down Catfish

DISTRIBUTION: Zaire

SIZE: Males 3¼in; females 4in

COMPATIBILITY: Peaceful with all but the smallest fish

6·5
▼
7·5 pH

pH: 6.5–7.5

dH: 8–15°

72°F
▼
79°F

TEMPERATURE: 72–79°F

BREEDING STRATEGY: Egg-layer

FOOD: Insectivore

S. nigriventris likes an aquarium planted with broad-leaved plants, but one that also has open areas for swimming. As its common names suggest, it spends much of its time inverted and for this reason its degree of pigmentation is reversed, the belly being much darker than the back. To make the fish feel secure, use floating plants or float a piece of cork bark on the water – the fish will rest beneath this when it is not out hunting for food.

Upside-down Catfish should be kept in schools. They feed inverted, taking insect larvae from beneath leaves and from the water surface. In captivity, they will eat most things and can often be seen feeding the right way up, taking flake or tablet foods from the substrate.

S. nigriventris has been bred in the aquarium. Females are more rounded and lighter colored than males. The eggs are placed in a depression in the substrate, and both the eggs and the subsequent fry are guarded by the parents. After absorption of the yolk sac, the fry should be fed on brine shrimp.

MISCELLANEOUS

BADIS BADIS
(HAMILTON, 1822)

FAMILY: Badidae

COMMON NAME: Badis, Dwarf Chameleon Fish

DISTRIBUTION: India

SIZE: 3¼in

COMPATIBILITY: Peaceful

6·5
▼
8·0 pH

pH: 6.5–8.0

dH: to 28°

TEMPERATURE: 72–79°F

72°F
▼
79°F

BREEDING STRATEGY: Egg-layer

FOOD: Carnivore

This attractive fish is a suitable subject for the community aquarium. Males are more brightly colored than females, and they have a concave ventral profile while that of the female is convex. Keep them in a well-planted aquarium with a sandy substrate and feed them on all kinds of small live foods such as *Daphnia*, *Tubifex*, mosquito larvae and bloodworms, and supplement this with finely chopped beef heart.

Their breeding strategy is similar to that of many cichlids. Provide an inverted flowerpot or a cave, and keep the water temperature at the upper end of the range. The male will embrace the female, and some 40–80 eggs will be laid in a cave. The male will guard them until they hatch, usually in about 72 hours, and continue to tend them until the yolk sac is absorbed. First foods should be newly hatched brine shrimp, and the size of foods can be increased as the fry grow. Once the fry are free-swimming, the parents should be removed or they may eat the youngsters.

BOTIA MORLETI
TIRANT, 1885

FAMILY: Cobitidae

COMMON NAME: Hora's Loach

DISTRIBUTION: Northern India, Thailand

SIZE: 3½in

COMPATIBILITY: Peaceful

pH: 6.0–6.5

dH: to 10°

TEMPERATURE: 75–82°F

BREEDING STRATEGY: Egg-layer

FOOD: Omnivore

6·0
▼
6·5 pH

75°F
▼
82°F

This is a crepuscular fish that spends much of the day hiding in secluded corners of the aquarium. Provide a soft sand substrate, because it likes to bury itself in it. Make sure that the plants are well established before you introduce the loaches, or the plants may be dislodged by the digging and tunneling activities of the fish. Because of their excavation work, it is important that all the rocks and wood are seated on the base glass of the aquarium to prevent them from being undermined and falling over.

The fish require soft, acid water, and this must be combined with subdued lighting and sufficient hiding places to give the loaches enough security to venture out on feeding forays. They love live foods – bloodworms, *Tubifex, Daphnia* and so on, and tablet foods will also be eaten, but often only as a last resort.

As with all *Botia* species, *B. morleti* has an eye spine. This bifid spine fits into a groove just beneath the eye, and the fish can erect it at will. They use it for defence. Take care when netting and handling the fish, because the spines are sharp and can cut you. When the fish are bagged for transportation, make sure that they are double-bagged and that the corners of the bags are taped up; otherwise, the fish may puncture them with their spines.

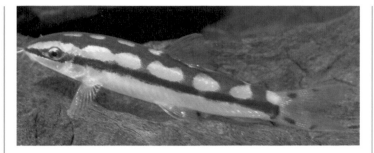

BOTIA SIDTHIMUNKI
KLAUSEWITZ, 1959

FAMILY: Cobitidae

COMMON NAME: Pygmy Chain Botia, Dwarf Loach

DISTRIBUTION: Northern India, northern Thailand

SIZE: 2¼in

COMPATIBILITY: Peaceful

pH: 6.5–7.5

dH: to 15°

TEMPERATURE: 77–80°F

BREEDING STRATEGY: Egg-layer

FOOD: Omnivore

6·5
▼
7·5 pH

77°F
▼
80°F

One of the most delightful little fish for the community aquarium, Pygmy Chain Botia should be kept as a school, when they will interact with each other. Keep them in a well-planted, well-filtered, mature aquarium with a fine sand or mulm substrate. They love to root about in the substrate for food. They can often be seen resting in groups on broad-leaved plants or on flat stones.

B. sidthimunki is not a fussy feeder and will accept flakes, tablet foods and small frozen foods, but there is no substitute for small live foods for bringing out the color and sheen on the fish.

There are no discernible sexual differences and, as far as is known, they have not been successfully bred in the aquarium.

Pygmy Chain Botia should not be introduced into newly set-up aquaria.

CHANNA OBSCURA
(GUENTHER, 1861)

FAMILY: Channidae

COMMON NAME: Snakehead

DISTRIBUTION: West and central Africa

SIZE: 14in

COMPATIBILITY: Predator

pH: 6.5–8.0

6·5
▼
8·0 pH

dH: to 20°

TEMPERATURE: 77–84°F

77°F
▼
84°F

BREEDING STRATEGY: Egg-layer

FOOD: Carnivore

C. *obscura* is a loner and is best kept on its own in a well-planted aquarium furnished with wood. The mottled brown coloration provides perfect camouflage among logs and branches as it lurks in wait for prey.

Feeding can be quite a problem, because very often these creatures will accept only live prey. With young specimens this is easy to overcome, as large insect larvae – dragonfly and water beetle – can be offered, but as the fish grows, the only alternative is smaller live fish. Even specimens of C. *obscura* that have grown up together have been known to become cannibalistic until only one or, if you are lucky, two, remain. It is rare for this fish to adapt to dead foods.

When breeding, between 2,000 and 3,000 eggs are produced and these are guarded by the male. After hatching, he continues his duties for another five days or so. The fry are cannibalistic.

GNATHONEMUS PETERSII
(GUENTHER, 1862)

FAMILY: Mormyridae

COMMON NAME: Elephant-nose

DISTRIBUTION: Nigeria, Cameroon, Zaire

SIZE: 9in

COMPATIBILITY: Territorial with its own kind

pH: 6.5–7.5

6·5
▼
7·5 pH

dH: to 20°

TEMPERATURE: 72–82°F

72°F
▼
82°F

BREEDING STRATEGY: Egg-layer

FOOD: Insectivore

Mormyrids have an electrical organ which they use for location, and this feature has also made them useful to man because they have been used to monitor water quality. Normally emitting 800 pulses a minute, this number increases as the fish become agitated by a decrease in water quality.

They are nocturnal and require an aquarium that has plenty of hiding places. They feed on live foods, such as *Tubifex*, *Daphnia* and bloodworms, which they take from the substrate. The best substrate for them is a fine sand so that no damage is done to their delicate snout. Elephant-noses will also accept flake foods, but it may take some time before they will accept them.

Some members of the family Mormyridae have been bred under captive conditions, but G. *petersii* is not one of them.

GYMNARCHUS NILOTICUS
CUVIER, 1829

FAMILY: Gymnarchidae

COMMON NAME: Aba

DISTRIBUTION: Senegal to Niger, Chad basin, upper Nile

SIZE: 3ft

COMPATIBILITY: Aggressive

6·5
▼
7·5 pH

pH: 6.5–7.5

dH: to 20°

73°F
▼
86°F

TEMPERATURE: 73–86°F

BREEDING STRATEGY: Egg-layer

FOOD: Carnivore

Abas are found in slow-moving, muddy waters and swamps. They have very small, almost redundant eyes, but they make up for their lack of vision by using a highly sensitive, weak electrical field. This is produced by an organ in the rear half of the body, which is situated on each side of the backbone; the head is positive and the tail negative. The fish detect any distortion of the field and hence locate objects and prey.

These creatures are interesting to observe under aquarium conditions because they can move just as easily backward or forward using undulating motions of their dorsal fin. They approach their prey cautiously and lunge at it only at the very last minute. They feed on insect larvae and small fish.

The only reports of breeding come from the wild, and they state that the eggs are laid in a floating nest of plant material. The parents guard the nest until the eggs hatch and the young leave it. At this time the fry are about 2in long.

GYRINOCHEILUS AYMONIERI
(TIRANT, 1883)

FAMILY: Gyrinocheilidae

COMMON NAME: Sucking Loach, Chinese Algae Eater

DISTRIBUTION: Northern India, Thailand

SIZE: 10in

COMPATIBILITY: Territorial

6·5
▼
8·0 pH

pH: 6.5–8.0

dH: to 25°

75°F
▼
82°F

TEMPERATURE: 75–82°F

BREEDING STRATEGY: Egg-layer

FOOD: Herbivore

This is probably the most commonly purchased algae eater for the community aquarium. The trouble is that the fish is not all that good at its job, and, being a somewhat boisterous and territorial creature, it will often uproot plants and harass other fish while defending its territory. It occurs naturally in mountain streams, where it uses its sucker mouth to hold onto rocks while grazing on algae. Because it cannot take in water through its mouth, the Sucking Loach has developed specialized gill slits. The water is taken in through two narrow openings in the nape region, reaches the gills via the pharynx, and is expelled through the lower part of the gill slits.

Although it is a herbivore, in captivity G. *aymonieri* is quite happy to feed on flake and tablet foods, pieces of chopped meat, small live foods and just about anything else.

Both males and females have spawning tubercules during the breeding season, and the female is much larger and more robust than the male.

LUCIOCEPHALUS PULCHER
(GRAY, 1830)

FAMILY: Luciocephalidae

COMMON NAME: Pike-head

DISTRIBUTION: Malay Peninsula, Singapore, Sumatra, Borneo

SIZE: 7in

COMPATIBILITY: Predator

6·5
▼
7·0 pH

pH: 6.5–7.0

dH: 8–10°

70°F
▼
75°F

TEMPERATURE: 70–75°F

BREEDING STRATEGY: Egg-layer

FOOD: Carnivore

L. pulcher is an extremely difficult fish to acclimatize to aquarium conditions. It is a predatory, surface-dwelling fish, which inhabits fast-flowing rivers and streams, so it is essential that you use power filtration and create a good flow of well-oxygenated water in the aquarium.

Experience has shown that they require a mature set-up that is well-planted with plants that reach the surface of the water and that is furnished with wood. For much of the time, *L. pulcher* will be found lurking beneath the vegetation at the surface. They are sensitive to movement near the aquarium and take fright easily, and if there is insufficient cover, they dash wildly around the tank. Initially they will feed only on live fish, large insect larvae or insects that hover just above the surface, and my own experience was that it was not until they had been in captivity for some 30 months that they even attempted to lunge at tetra tabs. When they attack their prey, the body is contorted, and the fish suddenly propels itself forward to lunge at the prey – it often misses.

L. pulcher possesses a labyrinth organ and lacks a swim bladder.

MONOCIRRHUS POLYACANTHUS
HECKEL, 1840

FAMILY: Nandidae

COMMON NAME: Leaf Fish

DISTRIBUTION: Amazon basin, Peru

SIZE: 4in

COMPATIBILITY: Predator

pH: 6.0–6.5

6·0
▼
6·5 pH

dH: 2–6°

TEMPERATURE: 72–79°F

72°F
▼
79°F

BREEDING STRATEGY: Egg-layer

FOOD: Piscivore

The South American Leaf Fish is one of nature's oddities and is a fish for the specialist. Its resemblance to a dead leaf is amazing: the strongly compressed body combines with the small barbel on the lower lip, and the red-brown coloration to give it amazing camouflage. When it is hunting, it drifts through the water just like a floating leaf until it is close to a school of small, unsuspecting fish. When it is close enough, it opens its cavernous mouth and the prey is drawn in by the vacuum.

A species tank is recommended for this species. The fish are predators, and adults can consume at least half their own body weight in food each day. The fry are even more voracious, eating their own body weight a day. Live fish is the staple diet of adults; in all the time I have kept these creatures, I have never seen them take dead food. If you do not feel you can feed live fish, do not buy a Leaf Fish.

It is possible to breed them, but it is not possible to tell male from female when they are not in the act of spawning. A clutch of some 300 eggs is laid on a leaf, stone or other flat surface, and these are guarded by the male until they hatch some four to five days later. You then have to provide enough live food for the fry as well as the parents.

PANTODON BUCHHOLZI
PETERS, 1876

FAMILY: Pantodontidae

COMMON NAME: Butterfly Fish

DISTRIBUTION: West Africa, Nigeria, Cameroon, Zaire

SIZE: 4in

COMPATIBILITY: Peaceful, but may eat smaller fish

pH: 6.5–7.0

dH: 8–10°

TEMPERATURE: 73–82°F

BREEDING STRATEGY: Egg-layer

FOOD: Carnivore

6·5 ▼ 7·0 pH

73°F ▼ 82°F

This is a suitable fish for a community of medium-sized creatures. Butterfly Fish are surface dwellers, where they cruise around in search of insects that fall onto the water.

Butterfly Fish will accept most flake foods from the surface. They are also partial to flies, spiders, daddy-longlegs, meal worms, maggots (as used for fishing bait), and fish. They have also been known to eat wasps without any ill effects. A novel way of feeding them flies is to float a plastic container of maggots in the aquarium and, as these pupate and eventually hatch, the Butterfly Fish will eagerly consume them. Make sure you have a tight-fitting cover glass, or your home or fish house will be full of flies.

In males the trailing edge of the anal fin is convex, and the central rays form a tube. In females the trailing edge of the anal fin is straight. Feeding is the key to successful spawning. The prospective parents require a wide variety of foods. The fish spawn over a long period, with about six eggs being produced at each pairing, until a clutch of some 100 or more have been produced. The eggs are lighter than water and float to the surface. At first they are transparent, but after a few hours they become dark brown and can be removed for hatching elsewhere. At 77°F they hatch in 36 hours, but the fry are very difficult to raise.

POLYPTERUS ORNATIPINNIS
BOULENGER, 1902

FAMILY: Polypteridae

COMMON NAME: Ornate Birchir

DISTRIBUTION: Central Africa, Zaire

SIZE: 18in

COMPATIBILITY: Peaceful

pH: 6.0–7.0

dH: to 11°

TEMPERATURE: 75–80°F

BREEDING STRATEGY: Egg-layer

FOOD: Carnivore

6·0 ▼ 7·0 pH

75°F ▼ 80°F

Although it is a large fish, *P. ornatipinnis* is relatively peaceful. Problems may arise if several are kept together and there are insufficient hiding places for them all. Birchirs require a sandy substrate, and the tank should have thickets of plants, with rocks and wood forming caves to provide shelter.

They are carnivores and will take live fish if the opportunity arises, but they are equally happy on a diet of chopped beef heart, prawns, lance fish, larger insect larvae and so on.

Sexing these creatures is difficult. The anal fins of males are believed to be larger than females, while the head of the female is reported to be larger than that of males, but presumably, in order to ascertain this, you need to be comparing fish of the same age and size.

Little is known of their breeding habits as they have spawned only rarely in captivity. Males initiate courtship, and the eggs are placed among plants. In the region of 350 eggs are produced, and they hatch within four days at 77°F.

These fish will jump, so make sure that you have a suitable cover on the aquarium.

DIRECTORY
of
marine fish

WRASSE

Wrasse are members of the family Labridae. They are found in marine waters all over the world from tropical regions through subtropical areas to the temperate zones. They have a single, long-based, dorsal fin which is composed of a spiny first section followed by a shorter, soft-rayed section. They have canniform teeth as well as pharyngeal teeth, with which they crush their food.

Juveniles and adults can often be confused as their coloration changes as they grow. Males and females can also be mistaken for members of a completely different species because they, too, may have different coloration or even different body form. This has led to a great deal of confusion in scientific circles as males, females, and juveniles of a single species could have been given different names. Sex reversal is also well-known among the labrids.

Many wrasse act as cleaner fish and take up station on the reef so that larger fish know where to go to have their parasites removed. The most well-known of these in the hobby is Labroides dimidiatus, the Cleaner Wrasse.

GOMPHOSUS VARIUS
LACEPÈDE, 1801

FAMILY: Labridae

COMMON NAME: Birdmouth Wrasse, Beakfish Wrasse

DISTRIBUTION: Indo-Pacific

SIZE: 10in

COMPATIBILITY: Peaceful

FOOD: Omnivore

G. varius is easily recognized by its elongated body and beak-like snout, features that give rise to the common name, Birdmouth Wrasse. Adult males are a beautiful peacock green with lighter green finnage, while females and juveniles are dull brown. Youngsters will often act as cleaner fishes.

In the aquarium they can be fed on *Mysis* shrimps, brine shrimps and other meaty foods chopped to a reasonable size. They are constantly searching around the aquarium, seeking tasty morsels from nooks and crannies and, as they also require some green foods in their diet, they will graze on any algae present.

LABROIDES DIMIDIATUS
(VALENCIENNES, 1839)

FAMILY: Labridae

COMMON NAME: Cleaner Wrasse

DISTRIBUTION: Indo-Pacific

SIZE: 4in

COMPATIBILITY: Peaceful

FOOD: Omnivore

This fish is a must for the marine aquarium. The Cleaner Wrasse provides a service to other fish: it cleans them of parasites, a service that is obviously appreciated as the larger fishes remain stationary, with their fins spread, while the Wrasse performs the task. However, when you purchase a Cleaner Wrasse, look at its mouth, as there is a False Cleaner Wrasse (*Aspidontus taeniatus*), which, instead of cleaning the fish, takes chunks out of it. *L. dimidiatus* has its mouth at the tip of its snout; *A. taeniatus* has an underslung mouth.

Cleaner Wrasse will also feed on flakes, live foods and finely chopped meaty foods. It is always active.

DAMSELFISH

These colorful, active members of the family Pomacentridae are found from the tropics to the temperate zone. Their dorsal and anal fins have both a spiny and soft-rayed section and, interestingly, the scaling extends onto the fin bases. They have a single nostril on each side of the head and their lateral line is broken.

They make ideal fish for the novice aquarist as they are hardy, will eat just about anything, and will tolerate nitrites in the water. They make excellent fish for maturing a marine system.

Damselfish are bred regularly in the aquarium and commercially. They spawn on rocks, and the males guard the eggs and fry. Problems do occur with feeding the young which will only accept the smallest of foods.

Care should be exercised when adding new damselfish to an established aquarium which already houses other damsels. They can be very territorial, so existing territories should be broken up by moving some of the tank decor before introducing the new fish.

CHROMIS CAERULEA
CUVIER, 1830

FAMILY: Pomacentridae

COMMON NAME: Green Chromis

DISTRIBUTION: Indo-Pacific, Red Sea

SIZE: 4in

COMPATIBILITY: Peaceful

FOOD: Omnivore

Green Chromis are lively school fish, and they should be kept as a group because individuals tend to pine away and die. Their bright green coloration makes them a welcome addition to the aquarium. The size given above is for wild specimens, in captivity they may attain only half this length. In the wild, they congregate in large schools of as many as several hundred individuals.

They will accept all kinds of small meaty foods, such as brine shrimp, as well as frozen and flaked foods, but they are sometimes a little reticent about feeding.

Spawning reports say that they breed among filamentous algae on the reefs, the male fanning and guarding the eggs until they hatch in about three or four days.

DASCYLLUS TRIMACULATUS
(RÜPPELL, 1828)

FAMILY: Pomacentridae

COMMON NAME: Domino Damsel, Three-spot Damsel

DISTRIBUTION: Indo-Pacific, Red Sea

SIZE: 4¾in

COMPATIBILITY: Territorial

FOOD: Omnivore

Once you have seen these jet-black damsels, you will realize immediately where their common names originate – from the white spot on each flank and the one on the head. However, these spots may fade with age. In addition, if conditions are not to their liking, the jet-black coloration becomes cloudy gray. They are hardy fish, but very territorial and may cause trouble in the aquarium.

They will accept most foods in the aquarium, ranging from chopped meaty foods to flakes and frozen foods. In the wild they would be eating small shrimps and crab larvae, so the inclusion of some live foods, such as brine shrimp and *Mysis* shrimps, in their diet is beneficial.

POMACENTRUS MELANOCHIR

FAMILY: Pomacentridae

COMMON NAME: Blue-finned Damsel

DISTRIBUTION: Pacific

SIZE: 3¼in

COMPATIBILITY: Can be aggressive

FOOD: Carnivore

This fish can be easily confused with the other yellow-tailed blue damsels, and in order to distinguish among them you have to look closely at the scales, because those of *P. melanochir* are edged with black. Take care over companions, because it can be pugnacious.

Feeding poses little or no problems. Initially, they may be fed chopped meaty foods, but they will quickly accept flakes, especially if there are other fish in the aquarium already eating flaked foods.

GROUPERS/SEABASS

Groupers are members of the family Serranidae and are, in the main, large fish which are only suitable for keeping in aquaria when they are juveniles. Furthermore, the juveniles exhibit far better coloration than the semi-adult or adult fish. However, there are one or two that grow to a more manageable size; Calloplesiops altivelis, – the Marine Betta – is certainly one of them.

For the most part they are deep-bodied fish with large mouths. Their dorsal and anal fins have a spiny first part. Most species have fully scaled bodies, and their lateral line runs continuously from the head to the tail.

They spend much of their time lurking in crevices and caves, and are only seen when they make forays for food. Although young specimens adapt well to life in captivity, it is sometimes necessary to feed them live fish.

These creatures have not been bred in the aquarium. Some species are known to be hermaphrodites; indeed, in some species, eggs and sperm develop simultaneously in the same fish. The fish are usually female when young, changing to males later on.

CALLOPLESIOPS ALTIVELIS
(STEINDACHNER, 1903)

FAMILY: Plesiopidae

COMMON NAME: Marine Betta, Blue-spotted Longfin, Comet Grouper

DISTRIBUTION: Indo-Pacific

SIZE: 6in

COMPATIBILITY: Peaceful with fish large enough not to be eaten

FOOD: Carnivore

One of the most endearing things about this fish is its ability to deceive. At first glance you have no idea which end is which. The light spots cover the entire surface area of the fish, surrounding the eye and effectively concealing it, while a large black spot surrounded by white provides a false eye at the rear and base of the dorsal fin. Predators usually strike at the eye of prospective prey to make sure that they have it head-on and any scales and spines will not stick in their throat. However, if they strike at the false eye of *C. altivelis*, they will only get a mouthful of finnage, and the Marine Betta will regrow its fin and live to fight another day.

Do not keep these fishes with smaller companions because they are carnivores and are not averse to eating them. They hunt with their heads down. Offer them live fish and meaty foods.

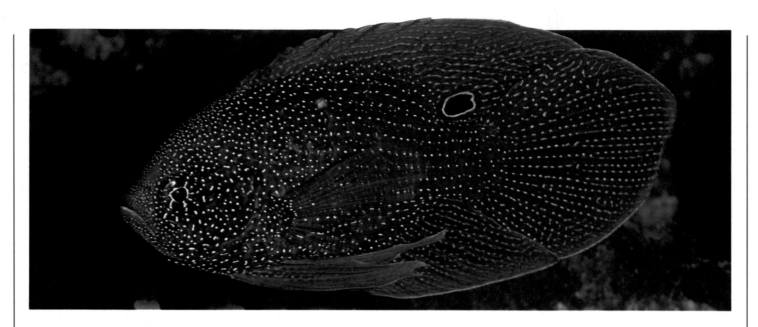

CALLOPLESIOPS ARGUS
FOWLER & BEAN, 1930

FAMILY: Plesiopidae

COMMON NAME: Marine Betta

DISTRIBUTION: Western Pacific

SIZE: 6¼in

COMPATIBILITY: Peaceful with fish large enough not to be eaten

FOOD: Carnivore

Not imported as frequently as *C. altivelis*, *C. argus* differs in having a lighter colored body with much smaller spots. However, their lifestyles are similar.

In the wild, *C. argus* feeds on small crabs and fish, and similar items should be offered in the aquarium. Although they will usually take only live foods when they are first imported, they can be weaned over to accept dead, meaty foods.

CHROMILEPTIS ALTIVELIS
(VALENCIENNES)

FAMILY: Serranidae

COMMON NAME: Pantherfish, Polkadot Grouper

DISTRIBUTION: Indo-Pacific

SIZE: 20in

COMPATIBILITY: Peaceful among fish of a suitable size

FOOD: Carnivore

environment, provide it with an extremely effective camouflage. As the fish matures, the pattern changes: the blotches become smaller but increase in number, so that it becomes a white fish with dark red-brown to black spots, which even extend into the fins.

Of all the groupers, *C. altivelis* is probably the best suited to the home aquarium as it is of managable size and, for a grouper, has a relatively small mouth. The coloration also makes it pleasing to the eye and, coupled with the fact that it is constantly out and about, it is an asset to any tank – or, at least any tank with fish that are not small enough to be eaten!

The color pattern changes a little from juvenile to adult. In small specimens, there are a few dark blotches on a light background, which, when the creature is seen in its natural

GRAMMA LORETO
POEY, 1868

FAMILY: Grammatidae

COMMON NAME: Royal Gramma, Fairy Baslet

DISTRIBUTION: Western Atlantic

SIZE: 4¾in

COMPATIBILITY: Peaceful

FOOD: Omnivore

Its striking coloration makes this an ever-popular aquarium fish, but these secretive cave dwellers require a quiet aquarium with no boisterous companions. Provide crevices and caves to give these fish the security they need, and you will often see them out and about in the tank. In the wild they are caught in caves and beneath ledges at depths of up to 200ft. Make sure that you have a good cover over the aquarium, because this fish jumps.

They will eat most things, from live shrimps to chopped meat, and including green foods and flakes.

They have been bred in captivity. In one report, the male is said to be larger than the female and to have lined a cave with algal threads before being seen to be incubating a mouthful of eggs, which later proved infertile. Another report states that nest-building using algal and small bits of staghorn coral was observed. Fry hatched, but they were not raised successfully.

LUTJANUS SEBAE
(CUVIER & VALENCIENNES, 1828)

FAMILY: Lutjanidae

COMMON NAME: Emperor Snapper

DISTRIBUTION: Indo-Pacific

SIZE: 3ft

COMPATIBILITY: Peaceful

FOOD: Carnivore

Small specimens settle easily to aquarium life, and as juveniles they are attractive fishes, their creamy white bodies being overlaid with three broad, red-brown bands. Unfortunately, as the fish grows, the color fades. Growth is rapid, and the Emperor Snapper will soon outgrow all but the largest of aquaria. They do, however, make excellent specimen fish for public aquaria. Large specimens can weigh up to 48lb.

They are carnivores and may be fed anything meaty. Make sure that their tank mates are large enough not to be swallowed.

Throughout its range, it is noted as a food fish. It is also noted as a sport fish because, having taken the bait, it puts up a tremendous fight. It is also caught by native fishermen in baited wire fish traps.

GRAMMA LORETO

LUTJANUS SEBAE

SYMPHORICHTHYS SPILURUS
(GUENTHER)

FAMILY: Lutjanidae

COMMON NAME: Majestic Snapper

DISTRIBUTION: Pacific

SIZE: 13in

COMPATIBILITY: Peaceful

FOOD: Carnivore

This is a good fish for the community aquarium as long as its companions are as big or bigger than it is. The main problem that may arise is that any fin-nipping fish in the aquarium will attack the fish's long, trailing dorsal and anal fin extensions. Do not keep it with smaller fish, as they may be eaten. The Majestic Snapper requires plenty of swimming space if it is to be seen at its best.

S. spilurus takes food readily, and all sorts of meaty foods, such as prawns, live river shrimp, mussels and lancefish, should be offered.

ANGELFISH

Angelfish belong to the family Pomacanthidae which contains some 74 species found throughout the tropical seas. The greatest concentration of species is in the western Pacific where 40 species have been found.

Angelfish are often confused with Butterflyfish (family Chaetodontidae), but can be most easily differentiated by the presence of a spine on the gill cover of the Angelfish. In addition, the larvae of chaetodontids are covered with bony plates which are absent in young pomacanthids.

Juvenile Angelfish exhibit differing color patterns from the adults, and the young of different species can easily be confused. Several are black with blue and white banding while others are black with yellow bands.

In the wild, Angelfish spawn at dusk. Pairs ascend through the water column, and the eggs and sperm are released simultaneously. The fertilized eggs float among the plankton for about four weeks before hatching. Some of the Dwarf Angelfish have been reared successfully in the aquarium.

CENTROPYGE ARGI
WOODS & KANAZAWA, 1951

FAMILY: Pomacanthidae

COMMON NAME: Cherub Angelfish, Pygmy Angelfish

DISTRIBUTION: Western Atlantic

SIZE: 2¾in

COMPATIBILITY: Peaceful

FOOD: Omnivore

Pygmy Angelfish inhabit stony areas below depths of 100ft, although they have been sighted in shallower regions, including a 1968 report of their being found among shell debris in the Bahamas at only 16–33ft.

They are small, hardy fish, which are well suited to the aquarium. Pairs may be kept together, because although they can be territorial, their territories are not very large.

They are easy to feed, but you must make sure that there is plenty of algae as this forms an important part of their diet. Small meaty foods and live shrimps may also be offered.

Fish from different localities will often exhibit variations in patterning around the head.

HOLACANTHUS TRICOLOR
(BLOCH)

FAMILY: Pomacanthidae

COMMON NAME: Rock Beauty

DISTRIBUTION: Western Atlantic

SIZE: 30cm/12in

COMPATIBILITY: Becomes aggressive with age

FOOD: Carnivore

Juvenile Rock Beauties are yellow with a blue-edged dark spot on the flanks. As the fish matures, this dark region expands, covering about 65 percent of the body.

These creatures are for the enthusiast. In the wild they feed on sponges, so it is quite a challenge to entice them to accept meaty foods and algae as substitutes. However, there are now sponge-based foods available, which may prove to be invaluable when keeping them in captivity.

HOLACANTHUS TRICOLOR

POMACANTHUS CHRYSURUS
(CUVIER, 1831)

FAMILY: Pomacanthidae

COMMON NAME: Ear-spot Angelfish

DISTRIBUTION: Northwest Indian Ocean

SIZE: 10in

COMPATIBILITY: Peaceful

FOOD: Carnivore

Little is known about this species as it is seldom offered for sale in the trade. Juvenile coloration is stunning: alternate blue and white stripes on a velvety black background run vertically through the body and into the fins. The caudal fin is yellow with a white bar near the base. At this stage there is no sign of the ear-spot that gives the fish its common name. As the fish matures, the coloration changes: the head becomes yellow with blue markings around the mouth, eyes and operculum, and the ear-spot begins to develop toward the back of the head near the start of the lateral line. The finer blue lines on the body begin to fade. In adult specimens, the ear-spot is black ringed with yellow. The lower part of the head darkens, and the blue markings seem almost iridescent. The yellow darkens and spreads over the top of the head. The white body markings now terminate about two-thirds of the way down the flanks.

In the wild this fish feeds on sponges and turnicates.

POMACANTHUS CHRYSURUS

POMACANTHUS PARU
(BLOCH, 1787)

FAMILY: Pomacanthidae

COMMON NAME: French Angelfish

DISTRIBUTION: Western Atlantic

SIZE: 12in

COMPATIBILITY: Peaceful, although juveniles may nip other fish

FOOD: Ominvore

Juvenile French Angelfish are particularly attractive. Their black bodies have vertical yellow bars, but as the fish grows, the markings change to an intermediate form in which the bands become pale and body scales start to develop white edges until, in the adults, the bands disappear completely, leaving a black fish with white spangles on the body and fine white dots in the fins.

Young fish are noted for the manner in which they clean other fish. Cleaning stations are marked out on the reef, and larger fish with wounds or parasites visit the stations for the juvenile angelfish to pick off the offending organisms.

French Angelfish are omnivores, and they will take green foods as well as meaty foods. They will often graze on algae in the aquarium.

Take care when you catch these creatures because they have a spine on the lower part of the operculum.

CLOWNFISH

Clownfish, or Anemonefish as they are sometimes known, are perhaps the most popular of marine aquarium fish. Their ability to live within the stinging tentacles of sea anemones gives them an air of mystery.

In the wild, groups of Clownfish will live commensally in a large anemone, and only the dominant male and female will breed. However, if the dominant female dies, the dominant male will change sex and breed with the next dominant male.

Although Clowns are naturally found with anemones, they will survive in captivity without one. But, if you want to see them at their best, it is wise to provide an anemone. In the aquarium these fish are best kept as pairs with an anemone per pair; otherwise, the resultant territorial disputes may end with subdominant fish being harrassed to such a degree that they hide all the time. Clownfish breed relatively easily in captivity and several species are now raised commercially.

AMPHIPRION CLARKII
— BENNETT, 1830 —

FAMILY: Pomacentridae

COMMON NAME: Clark's Anemone Fish, Yellow-tailed Anemone Fish

DISTRIBUTION: Indo-Pacific, Sri Lanka, Persian Gulf

SIZE: 4in

COMPATIBILITY: Territorial

FOOD: Omnivore

The color pattern and intensity of color on *A. clarkii* can vary greatly, the background ranging from bright orange to black. In nature, these fish live as adult pairs together with one or two juveniles to a single host anemone. They are found at depths of between 3 and 180 feet.

A. clarkii feeds on algae and zooplankton in the wild. In captivity they will take flake, live and frozen foods of suitable size – brine shrimp, *Mysis* shrimp and so on – and finely chopped meaty foods.

In the aquarium, provide suitable anemones, and with luck, the fish may breed. The eggs are laid close to the anemone and guarded by the parents. This species is also bred commercially.

AMPHIPRION OCELLARIS
— CUVIER, 1830 —

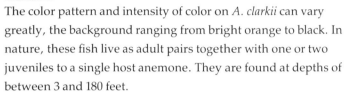

FAMILY: Pomacentridae

COMMON NAME: Percula Clown, Clown Anemone Fish

DISTRIBUTION: Indo-Pacific

SIZE: 35in

COMPATIBILITY: Territorial

FOOD: Omnivore

A. ocellaris is the most commonly imported of the clownfish and the one that everyone recognizes. It is often confused with *A. percula* but, according to some authors, it differs in the number of dorsal spines, the pectoral rays, the height of the spinous dorsal fin, and the width of the black edging to the white markings. Given that the range for both species overlaps, it is debatable whether the differences are sufficient to establish a new species or whether they are merely regional variants of the same species. There is also the problem of black version with white bars – where would it fit? The debate continues.

Provide an aquarium with several anemones, and, if you are keeping them with other clownfish, watch out for territorial disputes because *A. ocellaris* will defend its anemone against all comers. It will accept most live foods, finely chopped food and flakes.

A. ocellaris is bred commercially.

AMPHIPRION PERIDERAION
BLEEKER, 1855

FAMILY: Pomacentridae

COMMON NAME: Skunk Clownfish

DISTRIBUTION: Pacific

SIZE: 3¼in

COMPATIBILITY: Retiring

FOOD: Omnivore

These shy and retiring fish require either a quiet aquarium or a species aquarium, which is set up with several large anemones in which the fish can establish their home. In the wild they feed mainly on algae and zooplankton, and in captivity live foods, flake and finely chopped meaty foods are all acceptable.

In the wild they occur in mature pairs together with one or two juveniles at depths from 10–66ft, and mainly in association with *Stoichactis* anemones. Males may be distinguished by the orange edge on the soft part of the dorsal fin and the outer edges of the caudal fin.

The relationship between the clownfish and its anemone is not clearly understood, but there are many theories. The fish live in and near the anemone, and their body mucus is believed to protect the fish from the stinging cells. The anemone appears to protect the fish from predators, and it is possible that the anemone benefits from pieces of food that are dropped into it by the fish.

PREMNAS BIACULEATUS
(BLOCH, 1790)

FAMILY: Pomacentridae

COMMON NAME: Maroon Clownfish

DISTRIBUTION: Pacific

SIZE: 4in

COMPATIBILITY: Territorial

FOOD: Omnivore

P. biaculeatus is one of the larger clownfish. It can sometimes cause trouble in the aquarium because it is quite aggressive toward other clownfish. In the wild, it is usually found in pairs in protected, shallow areas 3–20ft deep, although it has also been observed at depths of 53ft. The female is the larger of the two fish.

In the wild these clownfish feed on zooplankton and benthic algae. In the aquarium offer finely chopped foods. They are greedy feeders once established.

The genus *Premnas* differs from *Amphiprion* in that it has smaller scales, an elongated spine below the eye, two predorsal bones (instead of the three found in *Amphiprion*) and fewer serrations on the cheekbones. It has a single species, *P. biaculeatus*.

LIONFISH/ SCORPIONFISH

The family Scorpaenidae contains approximately 60 genera with some 330 species, most of which are found in the Pacific and Indian Oceans. Only 11 genera with 58 species are found in the Atlantic. They are mainly bottom-dwelling fish, inhabiting rocks, coral reefs and kelp beds where they blend into the background; others bury in the substrate. So good is their camouflage that they are often trodden on by mistake. Their bodies are compressed and, if covered with scales, these are ctenoid. The dorsal, anal and ventral fins have spines and soft rays. The spines are equipped with poison glands which can inflict painful wounds on the careless handler or bather!

Many Scorpionfish are egg-layers, their eggs being deposited as a gelatinous balloon that in one species, Scoraena guttata, can be up to 8in in diameter. Other species, notably Sebastes, are live-bearers. It is of interest that those species found in cold, polar waters are more likely to be live-bearers than their tropical relatives, as in such areas free-floating eggs would soon become a meal for other creatures and would take far longer to hatch in the cooler temperatures.

PTEROIS RADIATA
CUVIER, 1829

FAMILY: Scorpaenidae

COMMON NAME: Whitefin Lionfish, Long-horned Lionfish

DISTRIBUTION: Indo-Pacific, Red Sea

SIZE: 10in

COMPATIBILITY: Peaceful with fish large enough not to be eaten

FOOD: Carnivore

This spectacular fish may be distinguished from *P. volitans* by the darker background color, narrow white bands, the horizontal bar at the base of the caudal fin, and the pinky-white snout and throat. The fin rays also lack the fleshy appendages of *P. volitans.*

P. radiata is nocturnal, and its white fin rays make it look quite ethereal as it drifts over the substrate in dim light. When it has become accustomed to captivity, it is quite happy to venture out during the day to feed.

Foods and feeding habits are the same as those of *P. volitans.*

P. radiata is also known by the name *Pteropterus radiatus.*

PTEROIS VOLITANS
LINNAEUS, 1758

FAMILY: Scorpaenidae

COMMON NAME: Scorpionfish, Lionfish

DISTRIBUTION: Indo-Pacific

SIZE: 14in

COMPATIBILITY: Peaceful with fish large enough not to be eaten

FOOD: Carnivore

This graceful fish requires careful handling, because the spines of the finnage have poison-producing tissue. If you are stung, bathe the affected area in hot water to reduce the effects of the poison and to relieve the pain.

Small specimens require live foods in the form of small fish, such as Guppies and Mollies, or shrimps. Once they are accustomed to captivity, it is possible to wean them onto dead, meaty foods such as lancefish. As hunters they are incredible to watch, drifting up to their victim before lunging at it.

Sometimes they will corner the food fish before lunging, and small specimens have been seen using this method to gang up on prospective prey.

P. volitans may be distinguished from *P. antennata* and *P. radiata* by its feathery pectoral fins, which have wider free rays, and the higher number of alternating bands on the body.

GOBIES

The family Gobiidae is the largest family of marine fish. Gobies, however, are a very diverse group of fish and are found worldwide in all waters, temperate to tropical, fresh, through brackish to marine. The family also contains one of the world's smallest fish, Pandaka pygmaea, *from the Philippines, which grows to about ¾in but is sexually mature at ¼in. Their well-developed ventral fins are joined to form an adhesive disk which allows the fish to cling to rocks and stones, and this is particularly important when you consider some of the habitats they live in, such as surge zones and mountain streams. When present, the first dorsal fin is spinous, the second composed of soft rays. Their scales are cycloid or ctenoid and are only rarely absent. Regardless of whether gobies are inhabiting muddy shores, tidal zones or the reef itself, all have their own hiding places to which they retreat when danger threatens. In order to make your fish feel secure, therefore, it is important to provide such retreats in the aquarium.*

Several species have been bred in captivity. Males and females may be differentiated by the size and shape of their genital papillae, which are shorter in males.

LYTHRYPNUS DALLI
(GILBERT, 1891)

FAMILY: Gobiidae

COMMON NAME: Catalina Goby

DISTRIBUTION: California – Pacific coast

SIZE: 2½in

COMPATIBILITY: Peaceful

FOOD: Omnivore

This is a beautiful little goby for the smaller marine aquarium. They are colorful fish and best kept as a group. They do not require such high temperatures as most marines, being quite happy with water that is below 72°F.

Most foods are accepted as long as they are of suitable size. However, live foods are particularly appreciated and may be necessary to bring them into spawning condition.

The Catalina Goby breeds quite readily in the aquarium, but raising the fry presents quite a challenge as they are very small. They spawn in burrows, caves or other sheltered areas, and the males guard the eggs.

This is a fairly short-lived species.

NEMATELEOTRIS SPLENDIDA

FAMILY: Microdesmidae

COMMON NAME: Firefish

DISTRIBUTION: Indo-Pacific

SIZE: 2½in

COMPATIBILITY: Peaceful

FOOD: Carnivore

N. splendida can sometimes be difficult to establish in the aquarium. You must make sure that there is a deep enough substrate to allow it to construct a burrow, for not until it has established its home will it settle down. It spends much time hovering just above the substrate looking for food, but, if it is threatened or disturbed in any way, will make a rapid dart for the safety of its burrow.

It is a colorful fish: the almost iridescent shades of blue, yellow and green are replaced with red on the hind part, which is the origin of its common name. The first rays of the dorsal fin are elongated, and the fish will often flick them in a flag-like manner.

Firefish will eagerly consume small crustaceans and other tiny live foods, and they may take frozen foods once they are established in the tank.

PTERELEOTRIS EVIDES
JORDAN & HUBBS, 1925

FAMILY: Microdesmidae

COMMON NAME: Scissortail

DISTRIBUTION: Indo-Pacific

SIZE: 5in

COMPATIBILITY: Peaceful

FOOD: Omnivore

P. evides is a bottom-dwelling fish that lives in a burrow, so you must provide a suitable sandy substrate some 3–4in deep. When they come out of their burrows, they hover just above the substrate, but they never venture far from the burrow in case danger threatens. For this reason, they are perhaps one of the most annoying fish to catch.

They will accept most foods, but in the first instance try live foods, such as brine shrimp. Later, offer chopped meaty foods and frozen foods.

MISCELLANEOUS

AEOLISCUS STRIGATUS
(GUENTHER, 1860)

FAMILY: Centriscidae

COMMON NAME: Shrimpfish

DISTRIBUTION: Indo-Pacific

SIZE: 4in

COMPATIBILITY: Peaceful

FOOD: Omnivore

This is an unusual fish. Its body is compressed and covered with armored plates, and all the fins are toward the rear of the body. What at first glance appears to be the caudal fin is, in fact, the dorsal fin, part of which provides the movable spine that is characteristic of the genus.

Shrimpfish swim in schools, adopting a head-down stance and using their anal and caudal fins to propel them through the water. A dark brown stripe runs the length of the body and through the eye, effectively concealing this delicate part of the fish's anatomy. Some reports say that Shrimpfish are found among the long dark spines of sea urchins, effectively camouflaged by the lateral black band, others state that they have been observed in caves, swimming in schools and working their way over the rock surfaces.

Reports also differ over their suitability for life in captivity. Some say they are easy and feed well on small shrimps such as brine shrimps and *Mysis*, while others state that they are not suitable and perish within a short time.

BALISTOIDES CONSPICILLUM
BLOCH & SCHNEIDER, 1801

FAMILY: Balistidae

COMMON NAME: Clown Trigger

DISTRIBUTION: Indo-Pacific

SIZE: 20in

COMPATIBILITY: Aggressive

FOOD: Carnivore

Triggerfish get their common name from their ability to lock the dorsal fin ray using a second ray. This is a defensive mechanism, and it serves to make their profile large should they be attacked by predators. In addition, the spine sticks in the mouth of the predator, preventing it from swallowing the triggerfish. When they are attacked or danger threatens, the fish retreat to crevices in the reef and lock themselves in using their dorsal spine.

Triggerfish also have a powerful set of teeth, which they use for eating mollusks and sea urchins – they will also nip at your fingers, so beware! Their trick of blowing at spiny sea urchins to turn them over to avoid the spines and then eating the unprotected underbelly is well documented. In the aquarium, triggerfish are voracious feeders and will eat anything and everything.

The Clown Trigger is an attractive fish, but it is also aggressive, so do not attempt to keep it with smaller fish.

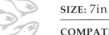

DUNKEROCAMPUS DACTYLIOPHORUS
(BLEEKER, 1853)

FAMILY: Syngnathidae

COMMON NAME: Banded Pipefish

DISTRIBUTION: Pacific

SIZE: 7in

COMPATIBILITY: Peaceful

FOOD: Carnivore

This elongated fish, attractively banded in red and white, is an oddity for the aquarium. It should be kept in a species aquarium or in a very quiet community aquarium. Like its close relatives the sea horse, the pipefish requires copious amounts of small live foods. The dorsal and pectoral fins are small and insignificant, but the caudal fin is highly colored and quite large.

In the wild, pipefish inhabit the crevices on the coral reefs. Their long snouts are ideally suited for extracting out small items of prey from such a habitat.

When these fish breed, the male carries the eggs around on the underside of his body.

CHELMON ROSTRATUS
(LINNAEUS, 1758)

FAMILY: Chaetodontidae

COMMON NAME: Long-nosed Butterfly Fish, Copperband Butterfly

DISTRIBUTION: Indo-Pacific, Red Sea

SIZE: 6in

COMPATIBILITY: Quarrelsome among their own kind

FOOD: Omnivore

Their striking coloration and black eye-spot in the upper hind portion of their body make Long-nosed Butterfly Fish easy to identify. They use their long snouts for feeding in nooks and crannies on the reef, and for picking out bits of food from between coral heads. They can be quite aggressive over territory in the aquarium.

Because of the size of their mouths, any foods have to be small – live brine shrimp and *Mysis* shrimp are taken – and the fish will eventually come to accept frozen foods and algae.

In order to keep these fish in good health, your system must be efficient, because they will be quickly affected by any slight deterioration in water quality.

HIPPOCAMPUS KUDA
(BLEEKER, 1852)

FAMILY: Syngnathidae

COMMON NAME: Yellow Sea Horse, Golden Sea Horse

DISTRIBUTION: Indo-Pacific

SIZE: 10in (height)

COMPATIBILITY: Peaceful

FOOD: Carnivore

Just about anyone who has ever kept a marine aquarium has probably wanted to try their hand with sea horses at one time or another. However, they require a species tank or a very quiet community aquarium, and you will need to provide anchorage points in the aquarium because sea horses use their prehensile tails to hold onto algae, coral branches and so on.

Feeding can sometimes be a problem, because they need tiny live foods such as brine shrimps, small crustaceans, *Daphnia* and newborn fry of live-bearers such as Mollies, Swordtails and Platies.

It is possible to breed sea horses in the aquarium. Males have a brood pouch, and the female uses her ovipositor to place the eggs into this abdominal pouch. The eggs are incubated for some four weeks until they hatch.

LO VULPINUS
(SCHNEIDER & MÜLLER, 1844)

FAMILY: Siganidae

COMMON NAME: Foxface, Badgerfish

DISTRIBUTION: Pacific

SIZE: 10in

COMPATIBILITY: Peaceful

FOOD: Omnivore

Members of the Siganidae family are known as rabbitfish, which refers to the rabbit-like shape of their faces. *Lo vulpinus*, however, has a much more elongated face, which terminates in a relatively small mouth. Rabbitfish require a surprising amount of vegetable matter in their diet, and the Foxface is no exception. In the aquarium they will also take frozen and dried food without too much trouble. The typical feeding pose for *L. vulpinus* is head down, grazing on algae.

Handle these fish with care because they are armed with poisonous spines on the dorsal and anal fins.

Some members of the Siganidae have been bred in captivity, but not this one. Males of *L. vulpinus* are generally smaller than females, and at breeding time the females are considerably fatter and have larger genital openings.

MONOCENTRUS JAPONICUS
(HOUTTUYN)

FAMILY: Monocentridae

COMMON NAME: Pinecone Fish

DISTRIBUTION: Indo-Pacific

SIZE: 6¼in

COMPATIBILITY: Species aquarium

FOOD: Carnivore

Pinecone Fish are deepwater fish, with an ancestry that stretches back for millions of years. They live in schools close to the seabed at depths of 120–600ft. The large, rigid scales are fused together, enclosing the body in a case. Each scale is edged in black and has a sharp spine at its center. The head is enclosed in a heavy bone case. There are a small pair of luminous organs containing symbiotic bacteria just below the lower jaw. It is believed that these are used to attract prey.

Although not often available as aquarium fish, these make excellent subjects for a species tank. They will accept small pieces of meat and fish, which should be chopped up.

The Japanese rear Pinecone Fish on a commercial basis. They are eaten roasted or fried with vinegar.

MYRIPRISTIS JACOBUS
CUVIER & VALENCIENNES

FAMILY: Holocentridae

COMMON NAME: Blackbar Soldierfish, Squirrelfish

DISTRIBUTION: Northern Florida, to Brazil; Caribbean

SIZE: 7in

COMPATIBILITY: Boisterous

FOOD: Carnivore

Squirrelfish need a large aquarium with plenty of free space because they can be very boisterous. They are nocturnal and have very large eyes so that they can cope with minimal light levels. During the day they hide in crevices in the reef, so make sure that the aquarium is suitably decorated. The dorsal fin is in two sections, the first is long and spiny, while the second is composed of soft rays and is triangular in shape. There are also spines on the gill covers.

M. jacobus may be easily identified by the dark bar just behind the operculum.

These creatures accept most meaty foods, such as chopped meat and fish, as well as shrimps and sometimes flake. Eventually they will even come out to eat during the day rather than persisting with their nocturnal habits.

MONOCENTRUS JAPONICA

MYRIPRISTIS JACOBUS

OXYMONOCANTHUS LONGIROSTRIS
(BLOCH & SCHNEIDER, 1801)

FAMILY: Centriscidae

COMMON NAME: Long-nosed Filefish, Beaked Leatherjacket

DISTRIBUTION: Indo-Australian archipelago, Pacific Islands (excluding Hawaii)

SIZE: 4in

COMPATIBILITY: Peaceful

FOOD: Carnivore

The Long-nosed Filefish is easily recognized by its striking blue-green body, which is overlaid with yellow-orange spots and bars. The snout is long and pointed so that the fish can feed easily on coral polyps. In the wild they live in shallow regions among the branches of staghorn corals and are extremely difficult to catch.

In the aquarium, provide coral branches for them to hide among. Feeding can be a problem, but substitutes can be found and they will accept brine shrimp. This is a fish for the enthusiast because it is very demanding and, without due care and attention, will not survive long in captivity.

PLATAX ORBICULARIS
(FORSKÅL, 1775)

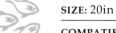

FAMILY: Platacidae

COMMON NAME: Round Batfish

DISTRIBUTION: Indo-Pacific

SIZE: 20in

COMPATIBILITY: Peaceful

FOOD: Omnivore

The compressed bodies and high fins of these fish are unmistakable, and the shape is highly suited to the species' normal environment of mangrove swamps. Their dull brown coloration also helps to camouflage them when they float like a dead leaf to avoid detection and capture.

Batfish grow large, and not only do they require a long, wide aquarium, but the depth of the tank must also be considered because the distance from the tip of the dorsal fin to the tip of the anal fin is usually far greater than its overall length. Provided they have enough space, they do well in captivity, feeding on just about anything from flakes and to live foods. Given the right conditions, growth is rapid.

OXYMONOCANTHUS LONGIROSTRIS

PLATAX ORBICULARIS

PLOTOSUS LINEATUS
(THUNBERG, 1787)

FAMILY: Plotosidae

COMMON NAME: Saltwater Catfish

DISTRIBUTION: Indo-Pacific

SIZE: 12in

COMPATIBILITY: Peaceful

FOOD: Carnivore

In its juvenile form, *P. lineatus* is very attractive: it has a black body with two white stripes running along its length. Young specimens are gregarious, and if they are not kept in groups in the aquarium, they tend to pine away. Unfortunately, as the fish matures, it not only loses its color and becomes a drab dark brown, it also becomes a loner.

Care is needed when handling any of the plotosid catfish. The dorsal and pectoral fin spines are poisonous. Should you have the misfortune to be stung, bathe the wound in hot water to help reduce the swelling and alleviate the pain.

P. lineatus will eat most meaty foods if they are cut up to a suitable size, and they may also take pelleted foods.

P. lineatus has been bred in the aquarium. The male guards the eggs and fry.

ZEBRASOMA FLAVESCENS
BENNETT

FAMILY: Acanthuridae

COMMON NAME: Yellow Tang

DISTRIBUTION: Pacific Ocean

SIZE: 8in

COMPATIBILITY: Territorial

FOOD: Herbivore

A perennial favorite for the marine aquarium, Yellow Tangs have a reputation for being aggressive and territorial, especially if two or three are kept together. Either keep one or keep a school of six or more individuals. These fish have a sharp, erectile spine on the caudal peduncle, which is used in combat and for defense. Take care when you are handling them.

Being herbivores, Yellow Tangs require copious amounts of algae in their diet. Allow algae to grow on the sides of the aquarium and under no circumstances attempt to keep these fish in an aquarium that is devoid of it. They graze for most of the day, and if there is insufficient green food in their diet, it must be supplemented by feeding lettuce.

The size given above is that of wild specimens; in captivity they may be expected to grow to 4–6in.

INDEX